INSTANT POT

Cookbook

1000 Days Instant Pot Recipes Plan Easy and Delicious Instant Pot
Cookbook With 36 Months Electric Pressure Cooker Meal Recipes for
Smart People

By Kathy Willson

or monetary loss due to the information herein, either directly or indirectly.

Respective authors own all copyrights not held by the publisher.

Introduction to Instant Pot

You are at a point in life when you know you need to make some healthy choices especially when it comes to your choice of food. The only problem is you can't seem to spare any minute to cook a nice and healthy meal when you get back home from work. The result? Takeout that you are genuinely so fed up of taking but the mere thought of fighting with pans and pots in your kitchen is almost unfathomable after a long and tedious day at work.

Well, this is where our Instant Pot Recipes come in. This book is here to show you that it is actually possible for you to make the healthiest meals for your family without breaking a sweat. It's as easy as combining all the ingredients of your meal in your instant pot and in a snap you have a hot and tasty dish ready and waiting.

Sounds too good to be true? Well, we haven't even gotten to the best part! You can prepare and cook all your meals in advance, say during the weekend or when you have some free time and once your food is ready, let it cool and pack it in your freezer. Come weekday, all you will need to do is take out your food, thaw it and you have a beautiful home cooked dinner. Forget about the frozen food from your supermarket, you can now make your own.

We will start by teaching you the basics of using an instant pot and why you need to have one, if you don't already have one; health benefits of following a vegetarian diet and lastly healthy vegetarian recipes that you can make for your family stress free.

Now, get your reading glasses, put your apron on standby and let's get into this cooking adventure!

Familiarizing yourself with the buttons of the Pot

The next step is to understand what the different buttons of your pot do!

- **Sauté:** You should go for this button if you want to simply sauté your vegetables or produces inside your inner pot while keeping the lid opened. It is possible to adjust the level of brownness you desire by pressing the adjust button as well. As a small tip here, you can very easily press the Sauté Button followed by the Adjust Button two times to simmer your food.

- **Keep Warm/Cancel:** Using this button, you will be able to turn your pressure cooker off. Alternatively, you can use the adjust button to keep maintaining a warm temperature ranging from 145 degree Celsius (at normal) to 167 (at more) degree Celsius depending on what you need.

- **Manual:** This is pretty much an all-rounder button which gives a greater level of flexibility to the user. Using this button followed by the + or − buttons, you will be able to set the exact duration of cooking time which you require.

- **Soup:** This mode will set the cooker to a high-pressure mode giving 30 minutes of cooking time (at normal); 40 minutes (at more); 20 minutes (at less)

- **Meat/Stew:** This mode will set the cooker to a high-pressure mode giving 35 minutes of cooking time (at normal); 45 minutes (at more); 20 minutes (at less)

- **Bean/Chili:** This mode will set the cooker to a high-pressure mode giving 30 minutes of cooking time (at normal); 40 minutes (at more); 25 minutes (at less)

- **Poultry:** This mode will set the cooker to a high-pressure mode giving 15 minutes of cooking time (at normal); 30 minutes (at more); 5 minutes (at less)

- **Rice:** This is a fully automated mode which cooks rice on low pressure. It will adjust the timer all by itself depending on the amount of water/rice present inside the inner cooking pot.

- **Multi-Grain:** This mode will set the cooker to a high-pressure mode giving 40 minutes of cooking time (at normal); 45 minutes (at more); 20 minutes (at less)

- **Porridge:** This mode will set the cooker to a high-pressure mode giving 20 minutes of cooking time (at normal); 30 minutes (at more); 15 minutes (at less)

- **Steam:** This will set your pressure cooker to high pressure with 10 minutes cooking time at normal. 15 minutes cook time at more and 3 minutes cook time at less. Keep in mind that it is advised to use this mode with a steamer basket or rack for best results.

- **Slow Cooker:** This button will normally set the cooker at 4-hour mode. However, you change the temperature by keeping it at 190-201 degree Fahrenheit (at low); 194-205 degree Fahrenheit (at normal); 199-210 degree Fahrenheit (at high);

- **Pressure:** This button allows you to alter between high and low-pressure settings.

- **Yogurt:** This setting should be used when you are in the mood for making yogurt in individual pots or jars

- **Timer:** This button will allow you to either decrease or increase the time by using the timer button and pressing the + or − buttons

The advantages of the Pot

As for the advantages of using an Instant Pot, the core ones are as follows:

- **Save both energy and time:** Since the pot is able to cook meals almost 70% faster when compared to other meals and cooking methods, this **Directions:** greatly minimizes the time taken. Since the pot is insulated properly, it also helps to minimize energy loss and lower down energy consumption.
- **Preserve the nutrients of the food while keeping things tasty:** Most traditional cooking methods require you to submerge your produces completely underwater, which greatly wash away the protein and vitamins. In Instant Pot however, very minimal amount of water is used that prevents this from happening.
- **Kills of harmful Micro-Organism:** Pressure cooker allows the internal temperature to reach extremely high levels where most bacteria and viruses are killed off. Even the tough to kill ones that are found on raw maize or corns.

Great Tips for Using Your Instant Pot

Prep in advance

If your mornings are usually busy, prepare everything that you are going to need for your meal the night before. When using an instant pot, your ingredients should ideally be at room temperature, or as close to it as possible. So, you can take out your ingredients from the fridge, immediately you get up in the morning and leave them to warm up for about 20-30 minutes before turning on your pot. Cook your meals in minutes before leaving. You'll come back to a healthy meal in the evening.

Trim excess fat

The beauty of using an instant pot is you don't need to add any oil to your meals, especially if they are meat based. They won't stick to the bottom for as long as there is enough moisture in the in the pot. Usually when you cook meat on the stove top, the fat tends to drain away on its own but this is not the case in an instant pot and if you don't trim off the excess fat, you may end up with pools of oil in your stew.

For a tastier and healthier result, trim off the excess fat.

Go easy on the soup

When cooking using an instant pot, the moisture doesn't evaporate since it cooks with a tightly sealed lid all through. When adapting a recipe that's typically cooked on stove top, it's advisable to reduce the liquid content by about a third. As a rule of thumb, the soup/ liquid should only just cover the ingredients. Otherwise, overfilling your pot with soup or liquid may lead to a leakage from the top and risk your food not cooking as well as it should.

When filling your pot with ingredients, don't go past the three quarter-way mark.

Thickening your sauce

The fact that soup doesn't easily reduce in an instant pot means that it also doesn't thicken. If you like your broth or sauces nice and thick, you can roll your meat chunks in flour before browning them and adding them to the pot or alternatively, you can add a bit of cornstarch-water mixture towards the end of your cooking. Add it within the last 5 minutes of cook time.

Don't be a peeping Tom

Instant pots are designed to do their own thing. All you need to do is add all your ingredients, seal the lid, turn it on and leave it to cook for the required period. If you keep checking the progress of your meal from time to time, then you are going to have to increase your cook time as every time you take out the lid, you release some heat. Needless to say, it's very dangerous to open the pot while the pressure is still high and also your meal won't be as glorious as it would have been had you trusted the instant pot to do its thing!

When to add ingredients

The best instant pot recipes, like the ones we are going to share in our next section, are those where most of the ingredients are added at the beginning of the cooking process. This leaves you with a lot of time to do your other things.

Chapter 1: Breakfast Recipes

Protein Packed "Cakes"

(Total Time: 10 Min|Serves:6)

Ingredients

- 6 beaten eggs
- 1 cup of shredded bacon
- 1 cup of baby spinach
- 1 cup shredded mozzarella
- 1 cup of chopped tomatoes

Directions

1. Beat the eggs in a bowl then stir in the cream cheese.
2. Add the bacon, spinach, mozzarella cheese and tomatoes and mix well until a nice batter forms.
3. Pour the batter into 6 muffin cups, dividing the mixture evenly.
4. Add the steamer inset and 1 cup of water to your Instant Pot.
5. Wrap the muffin tins with foil and transfer them to the pot.
6. Allow them to cook on HIGH pressure for 5 minutes.
7. Release the pressure naturally and serve. Enjoy!

Southern Breakfast Cornbread

(Total Time: 2 Min|Serves: 2)

Ingredients

- 1 cup water
- 4 ½ tbsp Flour
- 1/3 cup Cornmeal
- ½ tsp Baking Powder
- ¼ cup Milk
- 1 small Egg
- 1 tbsp Melted Butter
- ¼ tsp Sugar
- Pinch of Salt

Directions

1. Grease a small loaf pan with cooking spray.
2. Pour 1 cup of water into the Instant Pot and lower the trivet.

3. Combine all of the ingredients in a bowl - add a little bit more flour if your batter is too thin.
4. Transfer the batter to the greased loaf pan.
5. Place in the IP and close the lid.
6. Choose MANUAL and cook on HIGH for 12 minutes.
7. Do a quick pressure release by switching the pressure valve to "venting".
8. Serve when cooled completely.

Creamy Herbed Eggs
(Total Time: 10 Min|Serves: 2)

Ingredients

- 2 Eggs
- 2 tbsp Heavy Cream
- Pinch of salt
- Pinch of Cayenne
- Pinch of Pepper
- ½ tsp Basil
- ½ tsp Parsley
- ¼ tsp chopped Chives

Directions

1. Grease 2 small ramekins with butter or cooking spray.
2. Whisk together the eggs and heavy cream then divide between the ramekins.
3. Sprinkle with salt and cayenne.
4. Pour 1 cup of water into the IP and lower the rack.
5. Place the ramekins on the rack and close the lid.
6. Cook for 2 minutes on MANUAL.
7. Do a quick pressure release by switching the pressure valve to "venting".
8. Sprinkle with the herbs and serve.

Mashed Cauliflower and Potatoes

(Total Time: 20 Min|Serves: 4)

Ingredients

- 1 ½ cups of water
- 2 pounds of potatoes sliced up into 1-inch pieces
- 8 ounce of cauliflower florets
- ½ a teaspoon of salt
- 1 minced garlic clove

Directions

1. Add the water and potatoes to your Instant Pot.
2. Sprinkle the cauliflower florets over top.
3. Lock the lid and cook on HIGH pressure for 5 minutes.
4. Allow the pressure to release naturally.
5. Sprinkle salt on top and mash the whole mixture with a piece of raw garlic.

Simple "Hard" Boiled Eggs

(Total Time: 11 Min|Serves: 4)

Ingredients

- Pasture raised eggs (As many as you may need)
- 1 cup of water

Directions

1. Add 1 cup of water to your Instant Pot and place the steamer insert inside.
2. Place the eggs on top of the steamer pot.
3. Lock up the lid and cook on HIGH pressure for 8 minutes.
4. Quick release the pressure by switching the pressure valve to "venting".
5. Transfer the eggs to an ice bath and allow them to cool.
6. Peel the skin and serve!

Very Friendly Egg Roll Soup

(Total Time: 60 Min|Serves: 4)

Ingredients

- 1 tablespoon of ghee
- 1 pound of ground pastured pork
- 1 diced large sized onion
- 32 ounce of chicken broth
- ½ a head of chopped cabbage
- 2 cups of shredded carrots

- 1 teaspoon of garlic powder
- 1 teaspoon of onion powder
- 1 teaspoon of sea salt
- 1 teaspoon of ground ginger
- 2/3 cup of coconut aminos
- 2-3 tablespoon of tapioca starch

Directions

1. Set your pot to Sauté mode and add the ghee.
2. Allow the ghee to melt and add the ground pork.
3. Stir in the diced onions and sauté for a few minutes until the beef is browned.
4. Add the remaining ingredients to the pot and lock up the lid.
5. Cook on HIGH pressure for 25 minutes.
6. Do a quick release by switching the pressure valve to "venting".
7. To thicken the soup, whisk 2 tablespoons tapioca starch with ¼ cup of the cooking liquid.
8. Stir the mixture into the Instant Pot and press Sauté.
9. Cook until the mixture thickens then enjoy.

Cheesy Pepperoni and Spinach Frittata

(Total Time: 30 Min|Serves: 2)

Ingredients

- 1 ½ cups Water
- 4 Eggs
- Salt and Pepper, to taste
- 1 tbsp Olive Oil
- ¼ cup Ricotta Cheese

- 2 tbsp grated Parmesan Cheese
- ½ tsp minced Garlic
- ½ cup Spinach, packed
- 1/5 cup Mini Pepperoni
- 2 ounces grated Mozzarella Cheese

Directions

1. Pour 1 cup of water into the IP and lower the trivet.
2. Whisk the eggs with some salt and pepper.
3. Stir in the oil, ricotta, parmesan, garlic, and spinach.
4. Pour the mixture into a small greased baking dish.
5. Arrange the pepperoni on top and sprinkle with mozzarella.
6. Place the dish inside the IP then close and lock the lid.
7. Cook on LOW for 35 minutes then allow the pressure to vent naturally.
8. Serve and enjoy!

Breakfast Cinnamon Bread

(Total Time: 35 Min|Serves: 2)

Ingredients

- 1/3 cup Flour
- 1 tbsp Flaxseed Meal
- Pinch of Salt
- ¼ tsp Cinnamon
- ¼ tbsp Yeast
- 2 tsp Sugar
- 1/3 cup Hot Water
- 2 tsp Canola Oil

Directions

1. Combine the flour, flaxseed meal, salt, and cinnamon in a bowl.
2. Sprinkle the yeast and sugar evenly over the hot water.
3. Allow the yeast and sugar to sit for 5 minutes then add to the other bowl.
4. Stir in the oil and knead with your hands until a dough is made.
5. Grease a small loaf pan and transfer the dough to it.
6. Pour some water into the pot (1-2 cups will do) and add a splash of vinegar. Lower the trivet.
7. Place the loaf pan inside.
8. Close the lid and cook for 20 minutes on HIGH then do a quick release by switching the pressure valve to "venting".
9. Let cool before serving and enjoy!

Simplest Meatball Ever

(Total Time: 15 Min|Serves: 5)

Ingredients

For Meatball

- 1 and a ½ pound of ground beef
- 2 tablespoons of chopped fresh parsley
- ½ a cup of almond flour
- 2 pieces of eggs
- 1 teaspoon of kosher salt
- ¼ teaspoon of ground black pepper
- ¼ teaspoon of garlic powder
- 1 teaspoon dried onion flakes
- ¼ teaspoon of dried oregano
- 1/3 cup of warm water

For meatball cook

- 1 teaspoon of olive oil
- 3 cups of sugar-free marinara sauce

Directions

1. Take a medium sized bowl and add all of the meatball ingredients to it.
2. Mix well and form 15 meatballs by hand.
3. Add the olive oil to your pot and grease it well.
4. Set your pot to Sauté mode and allow the oil to heat up.
5. Add the meatballs balls and sauté until browned then hit Cancel.
6. Layer the browned balls carefully in the pot and pour marinara sauce over them.
7. Lock up the lid and cook on LOW pressure for 10 minutes.
8. Do a natural release and serve!

Butternut Squash Soup

(Total Time: 35 Min|Serves: 4)

Ingredients

For Soup

- 1 teaspoon of extra virgin olive oil
- 1 large sized chopped up onion

- 2 minced garlic cloves
- 1 tablespoon of curry powder
- 3 pounds of butternut squash, cut up into 1 inch cubes and peeled
- 3 cups of water
- ½ a cup of coconut milk

For Extra Toppings

- Hulled pumpkin seeds
- Dried cranberries

Directions

1. Set your pot to sauté mode and add the olive oil and let it heat up.
2. Add onions and sauté for about 8 minutes until tender.
3. Add garlic and curry powder and sauté for 1 minute more.
4. Stir in the butternut squash, salt, and water.
5. Lock up the lid and cook on HIGH pressure for 30 minutes.
6. Release the pressure naturally over 10 minutes.
7. Open the lid and blend everything into a puree using immersion blender.
8. Stir in the coconut milk and season with some salt and pepper.
9. Serve with a topping of dried cranberries. Enjoy!

Instant Scotch Eggs

(Total Time: 15 Min|Serves: 2)

Ingredients

- ½ pounds ground Sausage
- 2 Hardboiled Eggs
- ½ cup Breadcrumbs
- 1 tbsp Vegetable Oil
- 1 ½ cups Water

Directions

1. Divide the sausage into two portions and wrap each one around an egg.
2. Roll the wrapped eggs in breadcrumbs.
3. Place the wrapped eggs in a steamer basket and drizzle with oil.
4. Pour the water into the IP and lower the basket.
5. Close the lid and cook on HIGH for 7 minutes.
6. Do a quick pressure release by switching the pressure valve to "venting".

7. Enjoy!

Blueberry Cheesecake Pancake for Two
(Total Time: 50 Min|Serves: 2)

Ingredients

- 1 ½ cups Water
- ½ cup Flour
- ¼ cup Milk
- 2 tbsp Flaxseed Meal
- ½ cup Cream Cheese, softened
- 2 small Eggs
- 1 tbsp Sugar
- 1/4 tsp Vanilla
- ½ tsp Baking Powder
- Pinch of Salt
- 3 tbsp Blueberries

Directions

1. Pour the water into the Instant Pot and lower the trivet.
2. Whisk together all of the ingredients, except the blueberries, in a bowl until smooth and lump-free.
3. Fold in the blueberries.
4. Grease a small baking dish with cooking spray.
5. Pour the batter into the dish.
6. Place the dish inside the IP and close the lid.
7. Choose MANAUL and cook the pancake for 35 minutes on LOW.
8. Do a natural pressure release.
9. Enjoy!

Mind-Blowing Brussels
(Total Time: 10 Min|Serves:4)

Ingredients

- 1 tablespoon of chopped almonds
- 2 pounds of halved Brussels sprouts
- ¼ cup of coconut aminos
- 2 tablespoons of sriracha sauce

- 1 tablespoon of vinegar
- 2 tablespoon of sesame oil (Allow in Whole30 when used in small amounts)
- 1 teaspoon of red pepper flakes
- 2 teaspoon of garlic powder
- 1 teaspoon of onion powder
- 1 tablespoon of smoked paprika
- ½ a tablespoon of cayenne pepper
- Salt as needed
- Pepper as needed

Directions

1. Set your pot to Sauté mode and add the almonds.
2. Cook for a few minutes, stirring often, until just toasted.
3. Combine the remaining ingredients (except the brussels sprouts) in a bowl.
4. Add the Brussels to the pot then add the mixture from the bowl.
5. Stir well then sprinkle with almonds and lock up the lid.
6. Cook on HIGH pressure for 3 minutes.
7. Release the pressure naturally and serve. Enjoy!

Lemony Tapioca Pearls

(Total Time: 15 Min | Serves: 2)

Ingredients

- 1 ½ cups Water
- ½ cup plus 2 tbsp Milk
- 2 tbsp Lemon Juice
- ½ tsp Lemon Zest
- 2 tbsp Brown Sugar
- 1/3 cup Tapioca Pearls

Directions

1. Pour 1 cup of water into the Instant Pot.
2. In a small baking dish, combine the milk, lemon juice, zest, sugar, and tapioca.
3. Place the dish inside the IP.
4. Close the lid and cook on STEAM for 10 minutes.
5. Do a quick pressure release by switching the pressure valve to "venting".
6. Serve and enjoy!

Simple Instant Hardboiled Eggs

(Total Time: 10 Min | Serves: 2)

Ingredients

- 4 Eggs
- 1 cup of Water

Directions

1. Place the eggs inside a steamer basket.
2. Pour the water into the IP and lower the basket.
3. Close and lock the lid.
4. Set the IP on MANUAL.
5. Cook for 7 minutes on HIGH.
6. Press CANCEL and release the pressure quickly by switching the pressure valve to "venting".
7. Serve and enjoy!

A Rough Patch Potato Roast

(Total Time: 12 Min | Serves: 8)

Ingredients

- 1 and a ½ pound of russet potatoes
- ¼ cup of avocado oil
- ½ a teaspoon of onion powder
- 1 teaspoon of garlic powder
- 1 teaspoon of sea salt
- ¼ teaspoon of paprika
- ¼ teaspoon of ground black pepper
- 1 cup of chicken broth

Directions

1. Slice the potatoes into wedges.
2. Set the pot to Sauté mode and add the avocado oil.
3. Once the oil is hot, add potatoes to the pot and cook for 5-8 minutes.
4. Stir well then season with onion powder, garlic powder, salt, pepper, and paprika.
5. Stir in the broth then press the Cancel button.
6. Lock up the lid and cook on HIGH pressure for 7 minutes.

7. Once done cooking, do a quick release by switching the pressure valve to "venting".
8. Open the lid and adjust the seasoning to taste. Enjoy!

Cheddar and Bean Quesadillas

(Total Time: 20 Min|Serves: 2)

Ingredients

- 1 stick butter
- 2 Tortillas
- 1/4 cup shredded Cheddar Cheese
- 4 tbsp canned Black Beans
- 1 tbsp Salsa

Directions

1. Melt half of the butter inside your Instant Pot on Sauté mode.
2. Add one tortilla and top with half of the cheddar.
3. Place the beans on top and drizzle with salsa.
4. Top with the remaining tortilla.
5. Sprinkle with the rest of the cheese.
6. Top with the remaining butter.
7. Cook for 1 minute and flip over.
8. Cook for 2 more minutes, or until golden on both sides.
9. Serve and enjoy!

Cheesy Breakfast Bagels

(Total Time: Min|Serves: 2)

Ingredients

- 1 ½ cups Water
- 1 Egg
- ¼ tsp Baking Soda
- 1/8 tsp Salt
- 3/4 cups grated Mozzarella Cheese
- 2 tbsp Cream Cheese
- ½ cup Flour
- 1 tbsp melted Butter

Directions

1. Pour the water into the IP and lower the trivet.
2. Beat the eggs with baking soda and salt then stir in the cheeses.
3. Gradually mix in the flour then divide the batter in two bagels.
4. Cut the bagels in half and brush them with the melted butter.
5. Grease a baking sheet that can fit into the IP and arrange the bagels on it.
6. Place the sheet on the trivet and close the lid.
7. Cook on MANUAL for 15 minutes.
8. Do a quick pressure release by switching the pressure valve to "venting".
9. Serve with favorite toppings and enjoy.

All Natural "Sugar" Free Applesauce
(Total Time: 15 Min | Serves: 4)

Ingredients

- 12 medium sized apple diced and peeled
- Scant ½ cup of water

Directions:

1. Transfer the peeled and diced apples to your Instant Pot and add water.
2. Cut a piece of parchment paper into a large circle big enough to cover the apples.
3. Place the paper on top of the apples
4. Lock up the lid and cook on HIGH pressure for 10 minutes.
5. Release the pressure naturally and open the lid, discard the paper.
6. Use an immersion blender to blend the whole mix until smooth. Enjoy!

The Instant Pulled Pork Ragu

(Total Time: 50 Min|Serves: 4)

Ingredients

- 18 ounce of pork tenderloin
- 1 teaspoon of kosher salt
- Black pepper as needed
- 1 teaspoon of olive oil
- 5 cloves of garlic
- 1 (28-ounce) can crushed tomatoes
- 1 small sized jar of roasted red peppers
- 2 sprigs of thyme
- 2 pieces of bay leaves
- 1 tablespoon of chopped up fresh parsley divided

Directions:

1. Set your pot to Sauté mode.
2. Season the pork with salt and pepper.
3. Add oil to the pot and allow it to heat up.
4. Add garlic and sauté for about 2 minutes then remove to a bowl.
5. Add pork and brown for 2 minutes on either side.
6. Add the rest of the ingredients alongside the garlic.
7. Lock up the lid and cook on HIGH pressure for 45 minutes.
8. Do a natural release the discard the bay leaves.
9. Shred the pork using forks and garnish with parsley. Enjoy!

Very Fresh Pina Colada Chicken!

(Total Time: 30Min|Serves: 4)

Ingredients

- 2 pound of organic chicken thigh
- 1 cup of fresh pineapple chunks
- ½ a cup of coconut cream
- 1 teaspoon of cinnamon
- 1/8 teaspoon of salt
- 2 tablespoon of coconut aminos
- ½ a cup of chopped up green onion

Directions:

1. Add all of the ingredients to your Instant Pot except the green onion.

2. Lock up the lid and cook for 15 minutes at HIGH pressure.
3. Once done, allow the pressure to release naturally.
4. Open up the lid and stir well.
5. Mix the arrowroot flour with a tablespoon of water to make a slurry.
6. Add the slurry to your pot and mix well to make a thick mixture.
7. Set your pot to Sauté mode and wait until the sauce it just thick enough.
8. Garnish with some green onion and enjoy!

Mushroom and Onion Egg Cups

(Total Time: 15 Min|Serves: 2)

Ingredients

- 2 Eggs
- 4 tbsp Half and Half
- Salt and Pepper, to taste
- 1/3 cup diced Mushrooms
- 2 tbsp Diced Onion
- ¼ cup shredded Cheddar Cheese
- 1 ½ cups Water

Directions

1. Whisk the eggs with the half and half. Season with some salt and pepper.
2. Stir in the mushrooms, onions, and cheddar.
3. Pour the water into the IP and lower the rack.
4. Take 2 silicone muffin cups and pour the egg mixture into them.
5. Place the muffin cups on the rack and close the lid.
6. Cook on HIGH for 5 minutes.
7. Do a quick pressure release by switching the pressure valve to "venting".
8. Serve and enjoy!

Lightly Appetizing Chicken Balls

(Total Time: 30Min|Serves: 24)

Ingredients

- 1.5 pound of ground chicken
- 1 teaspoon of sea salt

19

- ¾ cup of almond meal
- 2 minced garlic cloves
- 2 thinly sliced green onions
- 2 tablespoons of ghee (for greasing hand)
- 6 tablespoons of hot sauce
- 4 tablespoons of butter (for frying)
- Chopped up onions

Directions:

1. Take a large bowl and add the chicken, salt, almond meal, minced garlic cloves and green onions.
2. Stir by hand until the mixture is well combined.
3. Grease your hand with ghee and shape the mixture into 2 inch wide balls.
4. Set your pot to Sauté mode and add ghee.
5. Carefully place the meatballs into your pot and brown them for a few minutes – you may need to do this in batches.
6. Take a bowl and add the hot sauce and butter - microwave it to make the sauce.
7. Add the browned meatballs to your pot again and pour the sauce.
8. Lock up the lid and cook them for 20 minutes on Poultry mode.
9. Once done, allow the pressure to release naturally.
10. Switch the pot to Warm setting and let stand for 10 hours.
11. Serve the balls over cauliflower rice or zoodles!

Carrot and Spinach Sausage-Crusted Quiche

(Total Time: 40 Min|Serves: 2)

Ingredients

- 1 tbsp Olive Oil
- ¼ Onion, diced
- 1 cup Baby Spinach
- 1 Large Carrot, grated
- ½ tsp minced Garlic
- 4 Eggs
- ¼ cup grated Mozzarella Cheese
- 1/3 pound Mild Sausage
- 1 ½ cups Water

Directions

1. Heat the oil in the IP on Sauté mode.
2. Add the onions and cook until soft, about 4 to 5 minutes.
3. Add carrots and spinach and cook for 2 more minutes.
4. Stir in the garlic and cook for an additional minute. Transfer to a bowl.
5. Whisk the eggs and stir into the bowl with the veggies then add the mozzarella.
6. Pour the water into the IP and lower the trivet.
7. Grease a small baking dish.
8. Roll out the sausage and press into the bottom of the dish.
9. Pour the egg mixture over the sausage.
10. Close the lid and cook on HIGH for 25 minutes.
11. Release the pressure quickly by switching the pressure valve to "venting".
12. Serve hot and enjoy!

Bacon Thyme Eggs

(Total Time: 15 Min | Serves: 2)

Ingredients

- 2 Hardboiled Eggs
- 2 Kale Leaves
- 2 Bacon Slices

- ¼ tsp Garlic Salt
- Pinch of Pepper
- 1 ½ cups Water

Directions

1. Peel the eggs and wrap them firmly in kale leaves.
2. Wrap the kale leaves in bacon slices and season with the garlic salt and pepper.
3. Pour the water into the IP. Lower the rack.
4. Place the eggs on the rack and close the lid.
5. Choose MANUAL and cook on HIGH for 5 minutes.
6. Do a quick pressure release by switching the pressure valve to "venting".
7. Serve and enjoy!

Blueberry Coconut Porridge

(Total Time: 10 Min|Serves: 2)

Ingredients

- 1 cup Water
- 1 tbsp Honey
- ½ cup Cashews
- ½ cup Coconut Flakes, unsweetened
- ¼ cup Pumpkin Seeds
- ½ cup Pecan Halves
- ¼ cup Blueberries
- 2 tsp Butter, softened

Directions

1. Place the cashews, coconut, pumpkin seeds and pecans, in a food processor.
2. Pulse until ground then transfer to your Instant Pot.
3. Add the remaining ingredients and stir to combine well.
4. Cook for 3 minutes on HIGH.
5. Do a quick pressure release by switching the pressure valve to "venting".
6. Stir and divide between two bowls. Enjoy!

Sassy Spaghetti Squash with Garlic and Sage

(Total Time: 20 Min|Serves: 4)

Ingredients

- 1 medium sized spaghetti squash
- 1 cup of water
- 1 small bunch of fresh sage
- 3-5 cloves of sliced garlic
- 2 tablespoon of olive oil
- 1 teaspoon of salt
- 1/8 teaspoon of nutmeg

Directions

1. Halve your squash and scoop out the seeds.
2. Add water to the pot and place a trivet on top.

3. Place the squash on the trivet, cut-side up, stacking them on each other.
4. Lock up the lid and cook on HIGH pressure for 3-4 minutes.
5. Take a skillet and place it over low heat.
6. Add sage and garlic with a bit of olive oil and sauté for 1 minute.
7. Once the cooking is done, allow the pressure to release naturally.
8. Take the squash out shred the flesh using a fork and transfer them into the pan.
9. Turn down the heat and sprinkle a bit of salt and nutmeg.
10. Stir well and enjoy!

Lovely and Healthy Beets

(Total Time: 20 Min|Serves: 6)

Ingredients

- 6 medium sized beets
- 1 cup of water
- Kosher salt
- Freshly ground black pepper
- Balsamic vinegar
- Extra virgin olive oil

Directions

1. Wash the beets well and slice them.
2. Add 1 cup of water to your pot.
3. Place a steamer insert on top of the pot and arrange the beets on top.
4. Lock up the lid and cook on HIGH pressure for 1 minute.
5. Release the pressure naturally.
6. Open up the lid and allow the beets to cool.
7. Season the beets with a bit of pepper and salt.
8. Add just a splash of balsamic vinegar and marinate for 30 minutes.
9. Add extra olive oil and serve!

Garden Quiche

(Total Time: 30 Min|Serves: 2)

Ingredients

- 1 ½ cups Water
- 4 Eggs
- ¼ cups Milk
- ¼ cup Flour
- ¼ tsp Salt
- ¼ tsp Pepper
- 1 tbsp chopped Parsley
- ¼ cup chopped Zucchini
- ¼ cup chopped Tomatoes
- 1 scallion, chopped
- ½ Red Bell Pepper, diced
- ½ cup shredded Mozzarella Cheese

Directions

1. Grease a small baking dish with cooking spray.
2. Pour the water into the IP and lower the trivet.
3. Whisk together the eggs, milk, flour, salt, pepper, and parsley, in a bowl.
4. Stir in the veggies and half of the cheese.
5. Pour the mixture into the dish and cover with foil.
6. Place on top of the trivet and close the Instant Pot.
7. Set it to MANUAL then cook on HIGH for 20 minutes.
8. Do a quick pressure release by switching the pressure valve to "venting".
9. Top with the remaining cheese immediately.
10. Serve and enjoy!

Jalapeno Egg Poppers

(Total Time: 20 Min|Serves: 2)

Ingredients

- 4 Eggs, beaten
- ½ cup shredded Cheese
- ¼ tsp Black Pepper
- ¼ tsp Garlic Pepper
- Pinch of Salt
- 1 ½ Jalapeno Peppers, seeded and chopped
- 1 ½ cups Water

Directions

1. Whisk together the eggs and seasonings in a bowl.
2. Add eggs and jalapenos and stir to combine.
3. Pour the mixture into 2 mason jars.
4. Pour the water into the Instant Pot and lower the trivet.
5. Seal the jars and place on the trivet.
6. Close the lid and cook on HIGH for 8 minutes.
7. Release the pressure naturally.
8. Let cool slightly before serving.
9. Enjoy!

Turmeric Diced Eggs

(Total Time: 15 Min|Serves: 2)

Ingredients

- 1 ½ cups Water
- 4 Eggs
- ½ tsp Turmeric
- ¼ tsp Lemon Pepper
- ¼ tsp Salt

Directions

1. Pour the water into the IP and lower the trivet.
2. Crack the eggs into a greased baking dish, making sure not to break the yolks.
3. Cover the dish with a piece of aluminum foil and place on top of the trivet.
4. Close the lid and set to MANUAL and cook for 4 minutes.
5. Do a quick pressure release by switching the pressure valve to "venting".
6. Transfer the eggs to a cutting board.
7. Sprinkle with the spices and dice finely. Serve and enjoy!

A Delightful Picnic Salad

(Total Time: 14Min|Serves: 6)

Ingredients

- 2.5 pound of russet potatoes all peeled up and cubed

Dressing

- ¾ cup of mayonnaise (Whole30 Recipe Given)
- Olive oil as needed
- 2 tablespoons of fresh parsley chopped up nicely
- 1 mined up dill pickle spear
- 1 rib of chopped up celery

Garnish

- ½ a teaspoon of paprika

- 1 and a ½ cup of water
- 4 large eggs

- ¼ cup of scallions
- 1 tablespoon of yellow mustard
- 1 teaspoon of House TOG Seasoned Salt
- 1 teaspoon of Sea Salt
- 1 tablespoon of Dill Weed

Directions:

1. Soak the potatoes in water for 30 minutes.
2. Place the potatoes and eggs in your steamer basket and place it in your instant pot with the water.
3. Lock up the lid and cook it for 4 minutes at HIGH pressure.
4. Take a large bowl and combine all of the dressing ingredients.
5. Once the pot is done cooking, perform a quick release by switching the pressure valve to "venting".
6. Place the eggs in a bowl of ice water.
7. Toss in the potatoes to your bowl of dressing and mix them gently.
8. Peel your boiled eggs and chop them up and add to the potatoes, mix again.
9. Cover the bowl and keep it in your fridge to chill until ready to serve.
10. Sprinkle with some paprika and serve

Absolutely Incredible Asparagus Soup
(Total Time: 50Min|Serves: 4)

Ingredients

- 1 tablespoon ghee
- ½ a cup of chopped onion
- 1 clove pressed garlic
- 1 cup diced ham
- 2 ½ cups chicken broth
- ½ teaspoon dried thyme
- 2 pounds asparagus, sliced

Directions:

1. Set your pot to Sauté mode and add ghee.
2. Allow the ghee to melt and add diced onion - cook for about 5 minutes until the onions are browned.
3. Add pressed garlic, ham, broth and simmer for 2-3 minutes.
4. Add thyme and asparagus and lock up the lid.
5. Cook on SOUP mode for 45 minutes.
6. Release the pressure naturally and enjoy!

Sausage, Tomato & Corn Breakfast

(Total Time: 30 Min|Serves: 2)

Ingredients

- ½ pounds Sausage Links
- 2 Potatoes, thinly sliced
- 8 ounces canned Creamed Corn
- ¼ Onion, diced
- 2/3 cup Tomato Juice
- Salt and Pepper, to taste

Directions

1. Place the sausage links in the Instant Pot.
2. Set it to Sauté and cook until they turn brown on all sides.
3. Add potatoes, corn, onion, and tomato juice.
4. Pour the tomato juice over and season with salt and pepper.
5. Close the lid and set the IP to RICE then cook for 6 minutes.
6. Release the pressure naturally.
7. Serve and enjoy!

Classic Cornmeal in the Instant Pot

(Total Time: 20 Min|Serves: 2)

Ingredients

- 2 cups Water
- ½ cup Yellow Cornmeal
- ¼ tsp Salt
- Pinch of Pepper
- 1 tbsp Butter

Directions

1. Place 1 ½ cups of water in the IP and bring to a boil on Sauté mode.
2. Meanwhile, whisk together the remaining water, cornmeal, salt, and pepper.
3. When the water starts to boil, stir in the cornmeal mixture.
4. Stir to combine and close the lid and cook on SOUP for 10 minutes.
5. Do a quick pressure release by switching the pressure valve to "venting".
6. Stir in the butter. Serve and enjoy!

Espresso Oatmeal

(Total Time: 25 Min|Serves: 2)

Ingredients

- ½ cup Milk
- 1 ¼ cups Water
- ½ cup Steel-Cut Oats
- 1 tbsp Sugar
- 1 tsp Vanilla Extract
- ½ tsp Espresso Powder
- 2 tbsp Whipped Cream

Directions

1. Combine the milk, water, oats, sugar, vanilla, and espresso powder in your IP.
2. Close the lid and choose MANUAL.
3. Cook on HIGH for 10 minutes.
4. Release the pressure naturally for 10 minutes.
5. Do a quick pressure release by switching the pressure valve to "venting".
6. Divide between 2 serving bowls.
7. Place on top or stir the whipped cream into the oatmeal.
8. Serve and enjoy!

Astonishing Cauliflower Rice

(Total Time: 20 Min | Serves: 4)

Ingredients

- 1 large head cauliflower
- 1 cup water
- 2 tablespoon of olive oil
- ¼ teaspoon of salt
- ½ a teaspoon of dried parsley
- ¼ teaspoon of cumin
- ¼ teaspoon of turmeric
- ¼ teaspoon of paprika
- Fresh cilantro
- Lime wedges

Directions

1. Wash the cauliflower and cut away the leaves – cut into florets.
2. Place a steamer rack into your pot and place the cauliflower florets inside.
3. Add 1 cup of water to the pot.
4. Lock up the lid and cook on HIGH pressure for 1 minute.
5. Once done, do a quick release by switching the pressure valve to "venting".
6. Transfer the cauliflower to a bowl.
7. Set your pot to Sauté mode and add oil, allow the oil to heat up.
8. Add the cauliflower back to the pot and mash with a potato masher.
9. Add some spices and season it well.
10. Give a nice stir and a squeeze of lime. Enjoy!

The Less "Stinky" Onion Soup

(Total Time: 30Min | Serves: 6)

Ingredients

- 8 cups of yellow onion
- 2 tablespoons of avocado oil
- 1 tablespoon of balsamic vinegar
- 6 cups of pork stock
- 2 bay leaves
- 2 large sprigs
- 1 teaspoon of salt

Directions

1. Set your pot to Sauté mode and add the onions with oil.
2. Cook for about 15 minutes.

3. Add balsamic vinegar to the pot, scraping the browned bits from the bottom.
4. Add stock, bay leaves, thyme and salt.
5. Lock up the lid and allow them to cook under high pressure for 10 minutes
6. Allow the pressure to release naturally.
7. Discard the bay leaves and thyme stems.
8. Blend the soup using immersion blender.
9. Transfer it to your serving bowl and enjoy!

Great Morning Guacamole as A Spread

(Total Time: 150Min|Serves:6)

Ingredients

- 1 large sized avocado
- ½ of a juice lime
- ¼ finely chopped red onion
- 1 pinch of salt
- 1 finely chopped sprig cilantro

Directions

1. Halve the avocado vertically and gently remove the pit.
2. Run a knife vertically and then horizontally into the flesh.
3. Take a spoon and scoop out the cubed avocado pieces from the skin.
4. Place them in a small bowl then mash well.
5. Mix in the lime juice, salt, red onion and cilantro. Serve!

Cheesy Breakfast Steak Rolls

(Total Time: 50 Min|Serves: 2)

Ingredients

- ½ pound Beef Roast, cut into chunks
- ½ tbsp Brown Sugar
- ¼ tsp Onion Flakes
  ¼ tsp Mustard Powder
- ¼ tsp Salt
- ¼ tsp Pepper
- ¼ tbsp Balsamic Vinegar
- 1 tbsp Butter
- ½ tbsp Worcestershire Sauce
- 2 Hoagie Rolls

- 2 slices Provolone Cheese
- 3/4 cup Beef Stock

Directions

1. Combine the beef, brown sugar, spices, vinegar, butter, and Worcestershire in your Instant Pot.
2. Close the Lid and cook on MEAT/STEW for 40 minutes.
3. Do a quick pressure release by switching the pressure valve to "venting".
4. Divide the beef between the rolls and top with the cheese.
5. Drizzle some of the cooking liquid over. Serve and enjoy!

Instant Breakfast Bread

(Total Time: 35 Min|Serves: 2)

Ingredients

- 2 cups Water
- 1 tbsp Vinegar
- ½ cups Flour
- Pinch of Baking Soda
- ¼ tsp Salt
- ¼ cup plus 1 tbsp Sour Milk
- 2 tbsp Seeds by choice

Directions

1. Grease a small loaf pan with cooking spray.
2. Pour the water and vinegar into the Instant Pot.
3. Combine the dry ingredients in a large bowl.
4. Slowly mix in the sour milk.
5. Knead with your hands until sticky dough is formed.
6. Transfer to the pan and top with the seeds.
7. Cover the pan with aluminum foil.
8. Place it in the IP and close the lid.
9. Cook on HIGH for 15-20 minutes.
10. Do a quick pressure release by switching the pressure valve to "venting".
11. Let cool before slicing. Top with favorite toppings and enjoy!

Multi-Grain Breakfast Porridge

(Total Time: 60 Min|Serves: 2)

Ingredients

- 1 ¾ cups Water
- 2 tbsp Buckwheat
- 2 tbsp Barley
- 2 tbsp Brown Rice
- 2 tbsp dried Beans
- 1 Yam peeled and cubed
- 3 tbsp Applesauce

Directions

1. Combine all of the ingredients, except the applesauce, in the Instant Pot.

2. Close the lid and set the IP to PORRIDGE.
3. Cook for 45 minutes.
4. Release the pressure naturally for 5 minutes.
5. Do a quick pressure release by switching the pressure valve to "venting".
6. Stir in the applesauce then divide between 2 serving bowls. Enjoy!

The "Stinking Rose"
(Total Time: 156Min|Serves: 4)

Ingredients

- 3 cloves garlic
- Drizzle of virgin olive oil
- 1 cup of water

Directions

1. Add water to your pot and place a steamer rack inside.
2. Slice the garlic and add to the pot.
3. Lock up the lid and cook for 6 minutes at HIGH pressure.
4. Once the timer runs out, release the pressure naturally.
5. Take the bulbs out using tongs and transfer them to a heat safe dish.
6. Drizzle a bit of oil and broil in your oven for 5 minutes. Enjoy!

Mashed Assorted Veggies
(Total Time: 15 Min|Serves:6)

Ingredients

- 2 teaspoon of extra virgin olive oil
- 1 cup of diced yellow onion
- 4 minced cloves of garlic
- 2 cups of diced potatoes
- 1 cup diced carrots
- 1 teaspoon of sea salt
- 1 vegan stuffed roast
- ¾ cup of vegetable broth
- 2 tablespoons almond milk
- ¼ teaspoon of ground black pepper

Directions

1. Heat the oil in the Instant Pot on Sauté mode.

2. Add onions and garlic and sauté them for about 1 minute.
3. Add potatoes, carrots and salt - mix them well.
4. Thaw the vegan roast and place it on top of your veggies.
5. Pour the vegetable broth over it.
6. Cover the pot and let it cook at high pressure for 8 minutes.
7. Quick release the pressure by switching the pressure valve to "venting".
8. Add almond milk and black pepper to the vegetables and mash the mix using a potato masher
9. Slice up the roast and serve with the mashed veggies!

Your New Breakfast Pal "The Boiled Egg"

(Total Time: 153Min|Serves: 5)

Ingredients

- Eggs as needed
- 1 cup of water

Directions

1. Pour 1 cup of water to your pot.
2. Place a steamer basket on top.
3. Add the required number of eggs to the pot.
4. Lock up the lid and cook on HIGH pressure for 8 minutes.
5. Let the pot cook the eggs and once done, quick release the pressure by switching the pressure valve to "venting".
6. Allow the eggs to cool and open up the lid.
7. Transfer the eggs to your fridge and allow them to cool.
8. Serve!

Spicy Monterey Jack Omelet

(Total Time: 20 Min|Serves: 2)

Ingredients

- 1 ½ cups Water
- 3 Eggs

- ½ cup Half and Half
- 1 Chili, diced
- ¼ tsp Cumin
- Pinch of Cayenne Pepper
- Pinch of Salt
- Pinch of Garlic Powder
- Pinch of Black Pepper
- ½ cup shredded Monterey Jack Cheese

Directions

1. Pour the water into the Instant Pot and lower the trivet.
2. Beat the eggs with all of the spices and half and half.
3. Stir in half of the cheese.
4. Grease a baking dish and pour the egg mixture into it.
5. Place the dish inside the IP and close the lid.
6. Cook on STEAM for 15 minutes.
7. Do a natural pressure release.
8. Top with the remaining cheese immediately.
9. Serve and enjoy!

Instant Breakfast Burrito

(Total Time: 20 Min|Serves: 2)

Ingredients

- 2 Eggs
- ¼ tsp Chili Powder
- 1/4 tsp Taco Seasoning
- ¼ cup diced Ham
- ½ cup cubed Potatoes
- ¼ Onion, sliced
- 2 tsp diced Jalapeno
- 1 ½ cups Water
- 2 Burrito Wraps

Directions

1. In a bowl, beat together the eggs and the seasonings.
2. Stir in the ham, potatoes, onion, and jalapeno.
3. Grease a baking dish that can fit into the IP and pour the egg mixture into it.
4. Cover with aluminum foil.
5. Pour the water into the IP and place the dish inside.

6. Close the lid and cook on HIGH for 13 minutes.
7. Do a natural pressure release.
8. Divide the egg mixture between the burrito wraps.
9. Wrap them up and serve.

Eggs and Smoked Salmon

(Total Time: 10 Min|Serves: 2)

Ingredients

- 1 tsp Olive Oil
- 1 ½ cups Water
- 2 slices of Smoked Salmon

- 2 Eggs
- 2 tbsp Heavy Cream
- 1 tsp chopped Chives

Directions

1. Grease two ramekins with the olive oil.
2. Pour the water into the IP and lower the trivet.
3. Lay a slice of smoked salmon in each ramekin.
4. Crack an egg into each ramekin and pour a tablespoon of cream over.
5. Cover the ramekins with foil and place in the IP.
6. Close the lid and set to MANUAL.
7. Cook on HIGH for 4 minutes.
8. Release the pressure naturally.
9. Serve sprinkled with chopped chives and enjoy!

An Old Fashioned Baked Potato

(Total Time: 25Min|Serves:4)

Ingredients

- 1 cup of water
- 2 pound of medium baking potatoes (finely washed and scrubbed)

Directions

1. Wash the potatoes carefully and add them to your pot.
2. Make sure to pierce the sides of the potatoes thoroughly using a fork.
3. Add a cup of water and pre-heat your oven to 450 degree Fahrenheit.
4. Lock up the lid and cook the potatoes for 10 minutes over HIGH pressure.
5. Allow the pressure to release naturally over 10 minutes.
6. Take tongs and take the small potatoes out and transfer them to the middle rack of your oven, bake for 10-15 minutes (turn the heat off).
7. Repeat with the large potatoes for 10 minutes (do not turn heat on again).
8. Serve with your favorite toppings. Enjoy!

Eggplant Olive Spread for Generations To Come
(Total Time: 23Min|Serves: 6)

Ingredients

- 2 pounds of eggplant
- 4 tablespoon of olive oil
- 1 teaspoon of salt
- ½ a cup of water
- 3-4 cloves of garlic
- 1 juiced lemon
- 1 tablespoon of tahini
- ¼ cup of black olives
- Few sprigs of fresh thyme
- Some extra virgin olive oil

Directions

1. Peel up the eggplant and slice half of it into thick rounds.
2. Roughly chop up the remaining eggplant.
3. Open up the lid of your pot and put it on Sauté mode with the olive oil.
4. Add the large chunks of your eggplant and sauté for about 5 minutes.
5. Flip them over and add the rest of the chopped eggplant.
6. Add water and salt.
7. Lock up the lid of the cooker and let it cook at high pressure for about 3 minutes
8. Once done, release the pressure naturally and open up the lid.
9. Fish out the garlic cloves and discard the skin.
10. Tip your pot to discard the brown liquid.

11. Take an immersion blender and add tahini, garlic cloves, lemon juice and black olives.
12. Puree the mix with an immersion blender.
13. Pour it in your serving dish and garnish with some thyme, dash of fresh olive oil and black olives. Enjoy!

Sausage and Ham Omelet

(Total Time: 45 Min | Serves: 2)

Ingredients

- 1 ½ cups Water
- ¼ cup Milk
- ½ cup grated Cheese
- ¼ cup diced Ham
- ½ cup ground Sausage
- 1 Green Onion, chopped
- 3 Eggs, whisked
- ¼ tsp Garlic Salt
- Pinch of Pepper

Directions

1. Pour the water into the IP and lower the trivet.
2. Whisk the remaining ingredients together, in a bowl.
3. Grease a baking dish and pour the mixture into it.
4. Place inside the IP and close the lid.
5. Set it to STEAM and cook for 30 minutes.
6. Let the pressure come down for 10 minutes.
7. Serve and enjoy!

Juicy Apple and Cherry Breakfast Rice Pudding

(Total Time: 20 Min|Serves: 2)

Ingredients

- 1 tbsp Butter
- ¾ cup Arborio Rice
- ½ cup Apple Juice
- 1 ½ cups Milk
- 2 tbsp Brown Sugar
- 1 Apple grated
- Pinch of Cinnamon
- Pinch of Salt
- 1/3 cup pitted Cherries

Directions

1. Melt the butter in your IP on Sauté.
2. Add rice and cook for 5 minutes.
3. Stir in everything else except for the cherries.
4. Close the lid and cook on HIGH for 10 minutes.
5. Do a natural pressure release.
6. Top with the cherries.
7. Serve and enjoy!

Mesmerizing Piccata Potatoes

(Total Time: 13 Min|Serves: 4)

Ingredients

- 2 cups of water
- 4 sliced up russet potatoes
- 2 tablespoons of ghee
- 1 julienned onion
- 1 sliced up red pepper
- A quarter cup of vegetable broth
- 2 tablespoon of fresh lemon juice
- ¼ of cup of parsley
- Salt as needed
- Pepper as needed

Directions

1. Add water to your cooker.
2. Add potatoes and lock up the lid and cook on HIGH pressure for 5 minutes.
3. Release the pressure naturally and drain the potatoes in colander.

4. Add ghee to the pot and allow it to melt on Sauté mode.
5. Sautee the onions and red pepper then toss in the potatoes, broth, and lemon juice.
6. Cook for another 5 minutes.
7. Remove the heat and toss in the parsley.
8. Add some pepper and salt as flavor.

Pear and Pork Loin Chops

(Total Time: 157Min|Serves: 4)

Ingredients

- 2 tablespoons of clarified butter
- 4 pieces of ½ inch t hick bone-in pork loin or rib chops
- ½ a teaspoon of salt
- ½ a teaspoon of ground black pepper
- 2 medium sized yellow onions peeled up and cut into 8 wedges
- 2 large Bosc pears, peeled up, cored and cut into 4 wedges
- ½ cup of unsweetened pear, cider
- ½ a teaspoon of ground allspice
- Several dashes of hot sauce

Directions:

1. Set your pot to sauté mode and melt in 1 tablespoon of butter.
2. Toss your chops into your pot and cook for 4 minutes.
3. Transfer the chops to a plate and repeat to cook and brown the rest.
4. Toss in your onion and pears in your pot and let it cook for 3 minutes for until the pears are lightly browned.
5. Pour in the cider the and stir the allspice, and hot sauce.
6. Nestle the chops in your sauce.
7. Lock up the lid and let it cook for about 10 minutes at HIGH pressure.
8. Quick release the pressure by switching the pressure valve to "venting".
9. Keep it there for 10 minutes to steam up your rice.
10. Unlock and serve.

Tre Colore Frittata

(Total Time: 25 Min|Serves: 2)

Ingredients

- 1 ½ cups Water
- 4 Eggs
- 2 tbsp Milk
- ¼ tsp Salt
- Pinch of Pepper
- 1 cup Baby Spinach
- ½ cup diced Tomatoes
- ¼ cup grated Mozzarella Cheese
- 1 Green Onion, sliced

Directions

1. Pour the water into the IP and lower the trivet.
2. Whisk the eggs along with the milk, pepper, and salt, in a bowl.
3. Grease a baking dish and pour the egg mixture into it.
4. Top with 1/3 of the eggs with tomatoes, the other third with the spinach, and the rest of the eggs with mozzarella cheese.
5. Place the baking dish inside the IP.
6. Close the lid and cook on HIH for 15 minutes.
7. Do a quick pressure release by switching the pressure valve to "venting".
8. Serve and enjoy!

Eggplant Tahini Toast with Olives

(Total Time: 30 Min|Serves: 2)

Ingredients

- 1 ½ cups Water
- 1 Eggplant
- 1 Garlic Clove
- 1 tbsp Tahini
- 1 tbsp Olive Oil
- 2 tbsp Lemon Juice
- A handful of Black Olives
- Salt and Pepper, to taste
- 4 toasted Bread Slices

Directions

1. Combine the water and eggplant in the IP.

2. Close the lid and cook on HIGH for 5 minutes.
3. Do a quick pressure release by switching the pressure valve to "venting".
4. Peel and transfer the eggplant to a food processor.
5. Place the remaining ingredients to the food processor, except the bread, and pulse until smooth.
6. Divide the mixture between the toast slices and spread evenly.
7. Enjoy!

Pumpkin Pie Oatmeal

(Total Time: 25 Min|Serves: 2)

Ingredients

- 1 tbsp Butter
- ½ cup Oats
- 1 ½ cups Water
- 1/3 cup Pumpkin Puree

- ½ tsp Pumpkin Pie Spice
- 1 tbsp Maple Syrup
- Pinch of Salt

Directions

1. Melt the butter inside the IP on Sauté.
2. Add the oats and toast for 2-3 minutes.
3. Stir in the remaining ingredients.
4. Close the lid and set the IP to MANUAL.
5. Cook on HIGH for 7 minutes.
6. Let the pressure drop down for 10 minutes.
7. Serve and enjoy!

Heart Warming Baby Carrots

(Total Time: 20Min|Serves:4)

Ingredients

- 1 pound of baby carrots
- 1 cup of water

- 1 tablespoon of clarified ghee

- 1 tablespoon of chopped up fresh mint leaves
- Sea salt as needed

Directions:

1. Place a steamer rack on top of your pot and add the carrots and water.
2. Lock up the lid and cook at HIGH pressure for 2 minutes.
3. Do a quick release by switching the pressure valve to "venting".
4. Pass the carrots through a strainer and drain them.
5. Wipe the insert clean.
6. Return the insert to the pot and set the pot to Sauté mode.
7. Add clarified butter and allow it to melt.
8. Add mint and Sauté for 30 seconds
9. Add carrots to the insert and sauté well.
10. Remove them and sprinkle with bit of salt on top. Enjoy!

A Gentle Early Morning Carrot Soup

(Total Time: 25Min|Serves: 2)

Ingredients

- 3 minced garlic cloves
- ½ of a chopped yellow onion
- 2 cups of vegetable broth
- 1 tablespoon of curry powder
- 1 teaspoon of cayenne pepper
- 5 medium sized chopped and peeled potatoes
- 8 peeled and chopped carrots
- 4 cups of water
- 2 cups of finely chopped fresh kale

Directions

1. Mince the garlic and chop the onions.
2. Add them to your pot alongside ¼ cup of water.
3. Set your pot to Sauté mode and sauté for about 5 minutes.
4. Add vegetable broth, cayenne, curry powder and give it a nice mix.
5. Add water and sauté for 2 minutes.
6. Add the remaining ingredients (excluding kale) and lock up the lid.
7. Cook on HIGH pressure for 8 minutes.

8. Release the pressure naturally.
9. Blend using an immersion blender until you have a soupy consistency.
10. Chop up kale and stir in. Enjoy hot!

Crustless Kale and Tomato Quiche

(Total Time: 35 Min|Serves: 2)

Ingredients

- 1 ½ cups Water
- 5 Eggs
- 3 tbsp Milk
- ½ Tomato, sliced
- ½ tsp Garlic Salt
- Pinch of Black Pepper
- 1 cup chopped Kale
- ½ cup diced Tomatoes
- 1 Green Onion, chopped
- ¼ cup grated Parmesan Cheese

Directions

1. Pour the water into the Instant Pot and lower the trivet.
2. Grease a baking dish that can fit inside your Instant Pot with some cooking spray.
3. Whisk together the eggs, milk, garlic salt, and black pepper then pour into the dish.
4. Place the kale, diced tomatoes, and green onions in it.
5. Sprinkle the cheese over and arrange the tomato slices on top.
6. Choose the MANUAL cooking mode and cook on HIGH for 20 minutes.
7. Press CANCEL and wait for 10 minutes before doing a quick pressure release.
8. Serve and enjoy!

Chorizo Pepper Jack Frittata

(Total Time: 25 Min|Serves: 2)

Ingredients

- 1 ½ cups Water
- 4 Eggs
- Pinch of Salt
- Pinch of Pepper

- ½ tsp dried Parsley
- 2 tbsp Sour Cream
- 1/3 cup ground Chorizo
- ¼ cup grated Pepper Jack Cheese

Directions

1. Pour the water into your IP and lower the trivet.
2. Grease a round smaller baking pan with cooking spray.
3. In a bowl, whisk together the eggs, salt, pepper, parsley, and sour cream.
4. Stir in the chorizo.
5. Pour the mixture into the greased pan.
6. Sprinkle the cheese over.
7. Cover the baking pan with aluminum foil and place inside the Instant Pot.
8. Close the lid and choose MANUAL.
9. Cook on LOW for 17 minutes.
10. Release the pressure quickly by switching the pressure valve to "venting".
11. Serve and enjoy!

Supreme Celery and Potato Soup

(Total Time: 45Min|Serves: 4)

Ingredients

- 1 tablespoon of clarified butter
- 1 tablespoon of olive oil
- 2 large sized leeks
- 1 large sized chopped up onion
- 1 pound potatoes, chopped
- 1 teaspoon of thyme
- 2 medium sized celery roots
- ½ at teaspoon of garlic powder
- 1 piece of bay leaf
- ½ a teaspoon of salt
- 6 cups of fat free low salt chicken broth
- 6 pieces of medium sized celery ribs chopped up
- ½ a cup of fat free half and half
- 1 teaspoon of salt
- 1 teaspoon of pepper
- 1 and a ½ teaspoon of lemon juice
- ¼ teaspoon of cayenne pepper

Directions

1. Set your pot to Sauté mode and add butter with oil and allow the butter to melt.
2. Add leeks and onion to your pot and allow them to brown up, should take about 5 minutes.
3. Stir in potatoes, thyme, celery root, garlic powder, bay leaf and salt.
4. Add broth then set the pressure to HIGH and cook for 10 minutes.
5. Quick release the pressure by switching the pressure valve to "venting".
6. Open up the lid and add celery stalks.
7. Cook on HIGH pressure for 4 minutes and quick release once done.
8. Add pepper, salt, lemon juice, cayenne pepper and fat-free half and half.
9. Discard the bay leaf and blend the mixture using an immersion blender.
10. Puree the soup in your pot.
11. Ladle the soup into serving bowls and serve hot!

The Best "Steamed" Chokes

(Total Time: 25 Min|Serves: 4)

Ingredients

- 2 medium sized artichokes
- 1 lemon sliced in half
- 2 tablespoons of homemade Whole30 Mayo (Recipe Included)
- 1 teaspoon of Dijon mustard
- 1 pinch of paprika

Directions

1. Wash the artichokes carefully and remove any damaged outer leaves.
2. Trim the spines and cut off the upper edge.
3. Wipe the cut edges using a lemon half.
4. Slice the stem (if present) and peel the stem and chop it up. Keep it for later use.
5. Add a cup of water to the pot and place the steamer basket on top.
6. Transfer the chokes to the steamer basket and squeeze a bit of lemon on top.
7. Lock up the lid and cook on HIGH pressure for 10 minutes.
8. Allow the pressure to release naturally and enjoy!

Almond and Apricot Oatmeal

(Total Time: 20 Min|Serves: 2)

Ingredients

- 2 Large Apricots, chopped
- 1 tsp Vanilla Extract
- 2 tbsp Almond Meal
- 2 cups Water
- 1 cup Rolled Oats
- 1 tbsp chopped Almonds
- 1 tbsp Maple Syrup

Directions

1. Combine everything but the chopped almonds in your Instant Pot.
2. Close and lock the lid.
3. Choose MANUAL and cook on HIGH for 3 minutes.
4. Do a quick pressure release by switching the pressure valve to "venting".
5. Divide between two serving bowls and top with chopped almonds.
6. Enjoy!

Feta and Leafy Green Egg Cups

(Total Time: 15 Min|Serves: 2)

Ingredients

- 1 cup Water
- 1/3 cup chopped Leafy Greens (Chard, Spinach, or Kale)
- 2 Eggs
- Pinch of Pepper
- 2 tbsp shredded Mozzarella Cheese
- 2 tbsp chopped Tomatoes
- 2 tbsp crumbled Feta Cheese

Directions

1. Pour the water into the Instant Pot.
2. Take two silicone ramekins and divide the leafy greens between them.
3. Whisk together the eggs and pepper in a bowl.
4. Stir the remaining ingredients.
5. Pour the egg mixture into the ramekins.

6. Place the ramekins inside the IP, on the rack.
7. Close and lock the lid.
8. Cook on HIGH for 8 minutes.
9. Release the pressure quickly by switching the pressure valve to "venting".
10.   Serve and enjoy!

Sautéed Mushrooms for A Healthy Morning

(Total Time: 8Min|Serves: 2)

Ingredients

- 4 pound of beef short ribs
- Generous amount of Kosher Salt
- 1 tablespoon of beef fat
- 1 quartered onion with its skin on
- 3 cloves of garlic
- Water

Directions:

1. Add the listed ingredients to your Instant Pot.
2. Lock up the lid and allow them to cook on HIGH pressure for 4 minutes.
3. Do a quick release of the pressure by switching the pressure valve to "venting".
4. If the sauce has reached your desired consistency, then serve!
5. Otherwise, set your pot to Sauté mode and allow the liquid to reach boiling point.
6. Take a bowl and mix ¼ cup of water and 2-3 tablespoon of corn starch.
7. Gently stir the mixture into the sauce.
8. Stir for 1 minute and serve!

A Happy Morning's Picnic Salad 2

(Total Time: 14 Min|Serves: 6)

Ingredients

- 2.5 pound of russet potatoes all peeled up and cubed
- 4 large eggs
- 1 and a ½ cup of water

Dressing

- ¾ cup of olive oil
- 2 tablespoons of fresh parsley chopped up nicely
- 1 mined up dill pickle spear
- 1 rib of chopped up celery
- ¼ cup of scallions

- 1 tablespoon of yellow mustard
- 1 teaspoon of House TOG Seasoned Salt
- 1 teaspoon of Sea Salt
- 1 tablespoon of Dill Weed

Garnish

- ½ a teaspoon of paprika

Directions

1. Soak the potatoes in water for 30 minutes.
2. Place the potatoes and eggs in your steamer basket and place it in your instant pot with the water.
3. Lock up the lid and cook it for 4 minutes at HIGH pressure.
4. Take a large bowl and combine all of the dressing ingredients.
5. Once the pot is done, perform a quick release and set it aside.
6. Place the eggs in your bowl full of ice water.
7. Toss in the potatoes to your bowl of dressing and mix them gently.
8. Peel off your boiled egg and chop them up and add to the potatoes, mix again.
9. Cover up the bowl and keep it in your fridge to chill. Serve with a sprinkle of paprika on top!

Early Bird Egg Roll Bowl

(Total Time: 15 Min|Serves: 12)

Ingredients

- 2 teaspoon of sesame oil
- ¼ cup of Teriyaki sauce
- ¼ cup of coconut aminos
- 2 teaspoons of minced garlic

- ½ a teaspoon of ground ginger
- 1 teaspoon of onion powder
- ½ a cup of chicken broth
- 4 cups of cabbage/ Cole slaw mix

- 2 cups of shredded carrots
- 1 can of Bean sprouts drained up and rinsed
- Salt as needed
- Pepper as needed

Directions

1. Take a medium sized bowl and add sesame oil, teriyaki sauce, aminos, garlic, ginger and onion powder.
2. Add broth to the pot along with the cabbage, bean sprouts and carrots.
3. Cover them with the sauce mix and stir well to combine everything well.
4. Lock up the lid and cook for about 7 minutes over HIGH pressure.
5. Do a quick release and stir well.
6. Season with some pepper and salt.
7. Enjoy!

Prosciutto Mozzarella Egg Muffins

(Total Time: 20 Min|Serves: 2)

Ingredients

- 3 Eggs
- Pinch of Pepper
- Pinch of Garlic Powder
- Pinch of dried Basil
- 4 Prosciutto Slices, diced
- ¼ Green Onion, chopped
- 3 tbsp shredded Mozzarella Cheese
- 1 ½ cups Water

Directions

1. In a bowl, whisk the eggs along with the pepper, garlic powder, and basil.
2. Divide the prosciutto, onion, and mozzarella, between 2 silicone muffin cups.
3. Pour the egg mixture over.
4. Pour the water into the IP and lower the rack.
5. Place the muffin cups inside and close the lid.
6. Choose MANUAL and cook on HIGH for 10 minutes.
7. Release the pressure quickly by switching the pressure valve to "venting".
8. Serve and enjoy!

Scallions and Eggs Rice Porridge

(Total Time: 45 Min|Serves: 2)

Ingredients

- 1 cup Water
- 1 cup Chicken Broth
- 1 tsp Sugar
- Pinch of salt
- ¼ cup White Rice

- 1 tbsp Olive Oil
- 2 Eggs
- 2 Scallions, diced
- 1 tsp Soy Sauce

Directions

1. Place the water, broth, sugar, salt, and rice, in your Instant Pot.
2. Stir to combine and close the lid.
3. Cook on PORRIDGE for 30 minutes.
4. Release the pressure quickly and transfer to a bowl.
5. Wipe the IP clean and add the olive oil in it.
6. Set it to SAUTE and cook the scallions for a minute.
7. Add the eggs and soy sauce and scramble well.
8. Cook until the eggs are set.
9. Stir in the rice and cook for 2 minutes, or until thickened.
10. Serve and enjoy!

Meat-Loaded Frittata

(Total Time: 45 Min|Serves: 2)

Ingredients

- 3 Eggs
- 1/4 cup Milk
- Salt and Pepper, to taste
- 2 Bacon Slices, diced
- 1/3 cup ground Sausage
- 1/4 cup diced Ham
- 1/3 cup grated Cheese
- 1 ½ cups Water

Directions

1. Whisk the eggs with the milk, and some salt and pepper.
2. In a greased baking dish, combine the bacon, sausage, and ham.
3. Pour the eggs over and give it a good stir.
4. Top with the grated cheese.
5. Pour the water into the IP and lower the trivet.
6. Place the baking dish inside and close the lid.
7. Cook on HIGH for 30 minutes.
8. Release the pressure quickly by switching the pressure valve to "venting".
9. Serve warm and enjoy!

Most Authentic Pepper Steak from The County Side

(Total Time: 25 Min|Serves: 4)

Ingredients

- 1 pound of Boneless Beef Eye of Round Steak
- 80 ounce of sliced mushroom
- 1 piece of sliced up red pepper
- 1 tablespoon of minced garlic
- 1 pack of onion soup mix
- 1 tablespoon of sesame oil
- 1 cup of water

Directions:

1. Add the ingredients to your pot.
2. Lock up the lid and cook on HIGH pressure for 20 minutes.
3. Release the pressure naturally over 10 minutes.

4. Serve the pepper steak and enjoy!

Hard Boiled Lazy Devils

(Total Time: 15 Min|Serves: 4)

Ingredients

- 8 large eggs
- 1 cup of water
- Guacamole
- Sliced Radishes
- Mayonnaise (Whole30)
- Furikake

Directions:

1. Pour the water into the pot and add the silicone steamer insert.
2. Gently arrange the eggs on top of the silicone steamer insert.
3. Lock the lid and cook for 6 minutes on HIGH pressure.
4. Once done, let the pressure release naturally and toss in the eggs into an ice bath.
5. Peel them up after about 5 minute bath.
6. Cut them in half and garnish them in various dressing, such as Guacamole and Sliced radishes or Mayonnaise and Furikake alongside some sliced Persian cucumbers

Flax Coconut Breakfast Pudding

(Total Time: 10 Min|Serves: 2)

Ingredients

- ¼ cups Flaxseeds
- 2 tbsp chopped Almonds
- 2 tsp Sugar
- ¼ cup Coconut Flakes
- 1 cup Almond Milk

Directions

1. Place all of the ingredients in your Instant Pot.
2. Stir well to combine and close the lid.

3. Choose the MANUAL mode.
4. Cook on HIGH for 3 minutes.
5. Do a quick pressure release by switching the pressure valve to "venting".
6. Divide between bowls and top with your favorite toppings, if desired.
7. Enjoy!

Peppery Paprika Poached Eggs

(Total Time: 15 Min|Serves: 2)

Ingredients

- 1 ½ cups Water
- 2 Eggs
- ¼ tsp Paprika
- 1 tsp Dill

- 1 tsp Parsley
- ¼ tsp Garlic Salt
- 2 tbsp chopped Bell Pepper

Directions

1. Grease two ramekins with cooking spray.
2. Pour the water into the Instant pot and lower the rack.
3. Crack the eggs into the ramekins.
4. Divide the herbs and spices between them.
5. Whisk slightly.
6. Top with bell peppers.
7. Place the ramekins on the rack and close the lid.
8. Select STEAM and cook for 5 minutes.
9. Release the pressure by switching the pressure valve to "venting". Serve.

Ham and Cheddar Hash Browns

(Total Time: 10 Min|Serves: 2)

Ingredients

- 1 tbsp Olive Oil
- ¼ cup diced Ham

- ½ cups Frozen Hash Browns
- 2 Eggs

- 2 tbsp Milk
- Salt and Pepper, to taste
- 1/4 cup grated Cheddar Cheese

Directions

1. Set the IP to SAUTE and heat the oil in it.
2. Add ham and cook for a few minutes.
3. Stir in the hash browns and cook for another 2 minutes.
4. In a bowl, whisk together the eggs along with the milk and some salt and pepper.
5. Pour the eggs over the hash browns and give it a stir.
6. Close the lid and cook on MANUAL for 5 minutes.
7. Do a quick pressure release by switching the pressure valve to "venting".
8. Enjoy!

The Mediterranean Zoodles with Tuna
(Total Time: 15 Min|Serves: 8)

Ingredients

- 1 tablespoon of oil
- ½ a cup of chopped red onion
- 8 ounce of zucchini zoodles
- 1 can of diced tomatoes, basil, garlic , oregano
- ¼ teaspoon of salt
- 1/8 teaspoon of pepper
- 1 and a ¼ cup of water
- 1 jar of marinated artichoke hearts
- 1 can of tuna fish
- Freshly chopped up parsley

Directions:

1. Set your cooker to Sauté mode and cook the red onions for 2 minutes.
2. Toss in the zucchini noodles, tomatoes, salt and pour your water.
3. Let your pressure cooker cook at high pressure for 10 minutes.
4. Release the pressure naturally and open the lid.
5. Toss in the artichokes, tuna and any left-over liquid from the artichoke and sauté it on normal mode while making sure to keep stirring it for 5 minutes until very hot.

6. Serve.

Very Smoky Magical Chicken Sausage Soup

(Total Time: 40 Min|Serves: 6)

Ingredients

- 1 tablespoon of coconut oil
- 1 pound of boneless and skinless chicken thigh
- 1 pound of Andouille pork sausage
- 1 medium sized white onion
- 3 bell peppers
- 6 cups of chopped tomatoes
- 2 stalks of celery
- 2 large sized carrots
- 2 cups of bone broth
- ¼ cup of parsley
- 6 cloves of garlic
- 1 teaspoon of salt
- 1 teaspoon of thyme
- ½ a teaspoon of smoked paprika
- ½ a teaspoon of crushed red chili flakes
- ¼ teaspoon of black pepper
- ¼ teaspoon of cayenne
- 1 piece of bay leaf

Directions:

1. Add coconut oil to the bottom of your pot on sauté mode and allow it to heat up.
2. Add the sausage and chicken and cook until browned.
3. Slice up the onion and dice the bell peppers, chop the carrots and celery as well.
4. Remove the meat from your pot and keep it on the side.
5. Sauté the veggies by adding them to the pot.
6. Mince the garlic and add them to the pan.
7. Add broth and chopped up tomatoes then bring the whole mix to a simmer.
8. Once the chicken and sausage are cool, slice them up into bite sized portions and add them to the pot with the spices and parsley.
9. Give the whole stew a stir and lock up the lid.
10. Cook the stew in stew/soup setting for about 5-10 minutes.
11. Allow the pressure to release naturally.
12. Serve warm with some hot sauce if required.

Pomegranate Oat Porridge

(Total Time: 10 Min|Serves: 2)

Ingredients

- 1 cup Oats
- ¾ cup Water
- ¾ cup Pomegranate Juice
- ¼ tsp Vanilla Extract
- 2 tbsp Pomegranate Molasses

Directions

1. Combine the oats, water, pomegranate juice, and vanilla, in your Instant Pot.
2. Close the lid and choose MANUAL.
3. Cook on HIGH for 3 ½ minutes.
4. Release the pressure quickly by switching the pressure valve to "venting".
5. Divide the porridge between two bowls.
6. Top with pomegranate molasses.
7. Serve and enjoy!

Bacon Scramble

(Total Time: 15 Min|Serves: 2)

Ingredients

- 2 Bacon Slices, diced
- 4 Eggs
- 1/4 cup Milk
- Pinch of Pepper
- ¼ tsp Salt
- Pinch of Paprika
- Pinch of Cayenne Pepper
- ½ tsp dried Parsley

Directions

1. Set the Instant Pot to SAUTE and add the bacon slices in it.
2. Cook the bacon until crispy.
3. Meanwhile, whisk together the remaining ingredients.
4. Pour the eggs over the bacon.

5. Scramble with a wooden spoon and cook until the eggs reach your desired consistency.
6. Serve immediately and enjoy!

Italian Sausages with Peppers

(Total Time: 45 Min|Serves: 2)

Ingredients

- 14 ounces canned diced Tomatoes
- 4 small Italian Sausages
- 2 Green Bell Peppers
- 1 tsp dried Basil

- 7 ounces Tomato Sauce
- 1/2 tbsp Italian Seasoning
- 1 Garlic Clove, minced
- 1 ½ cups Water

Directions

1. Pour the water into the IP and lower the rack.
2. Place all of the ingredients in a baking dish that can fit into the Instant Pot.
3. Stir to combine well.
4. Place the dish inside the IP and close the lid.
5. Choose MANUAL and cook on HIGH for 25 minutes.
6. Let the pressure drop for 10 minutes.
7. Serve and enjoy!

A Beef Stew From The Renaissance

(Total Time: 45Min|Serves: 6)

Ingredients

- 16 ounce of tenderloin cut
- 1 tablespoon olive oil
- 1 piece of chopped onion
- 1 chopped zucchini
- 3 Yukon gold potatoes chopped up

- 1 cup of chopped carrots
- 2 cups of beef broth
- 1-2 teaspoon of sea salt
- 1 piece of bay leaf

- 1 teaspoon of pepper
- 1 teaspoon of paprika
- 1 teaspoon of onion powder
- 1 tablespoon of tomato paste
- Worcestershire sauce
- 2 tablespoon of arrowroot flour

Directions

1. Select the Sauté mode of your pot and carefully add tenderloin and oil.
2. Sauté until the meat is no longer pink then add the rest of the veggies.
3. Stir well and add the broth alongside the seasoning.
4. Stir well and choose the "Stew/Meat" setting.
5. Allow them to cook at high pressure for 35 minutes.
6. Once done, release the pressure naturally and let it rest for about 20 minutes on "Warm" setting.
7. Open up the lid and ladle ¼ of the liquid to a small sized bowl and add the arrowroot flour.
8. Mix well and add the slurry back to the soup to thicken it.
9. Add some salt if you need and serve!

Simple Mashed (Only) Cauliflower

(Total Time: 7 Min | Serves: 4)

Ingredients

- 1 large cauliflower head
- 1 cup of water
- 1 tablespoon of clarified butter
- 1/8 teaspoon of salt
- 1/8 teaspoon of pepper
- ¼ teaspoon of garlic powder
- 1 handful of chives

Directions

1. Core your cauliflower carefully into large chunks.
2. Add your steamer basket on top of your Instant Pot and add the cauliflower.
3. Add water to the pot.
4. Lock up the lid and allow it to cook for about 3-5 minutes over HIGH pressure.
5. Quick release the pressure by switching the pressure valve to "venting".
6. Remove the inner pot and drain the water.
7. Return the cauliflower to the inner pot.

8. Add butter and seasoning then puree everything with an immersion blender.
9. Stir and serve!

Braised Drumsticks for Every Morning

(Total Time:30 Min|Serves:6)

Ingredients

- 6 pieces of chicken drumstick
- 1 tablespoon of cider vinegar
- 1 teaspoon of kosher salt
- 1/8 teaspoon of black pepper
- 1 teaspoon of dried oregano

- 1 teaspoon of olive oil
- 1 and a ½ cups of jarred tomatillo sauce
- ¼ cup of chopped up cilantro
- 1 halved and seeded jalapeno

Directions

1. Season the chicken with vinegar, pepper, salt, and oregano
2. Allow it to marinate for a few hours.
3. Set your pot to Sauté mode and add oil, allow the oil to heat up.
4. Add chicken and brown it for about 4 minutes.
5. Add cilantro, jalapeno and salsa.
6. Cover the lid and cook on HIGH pressure for 20 minutes until the chicken is tender.
7. Release the pressure naturally.
8. Garnish with a bit of cilantro and serve!

Pleasurable Shepherd's Pie

(Total Time: 15 Min|Serves: 4)

Ingredients

- 1 cup of diced onion
- ½ a cup of diced carrot
- 1/3 cup of diced celery
- ½ a cup of diced turnip

- 1 teaspoon of bay leaf
- ½ a teaspoon of fresh rosemary
- 1 and a ¾ cup of vegetable stock

- 1 to 2 tablespoon of vegan Worcestershire sauce
- 1 to 2 teaspoon of tamari
- 1 cup of diced/canned tomatoes
- 1 tablespoon of tomato paste
- 1 portion of garlic mashed potatoes (recipe below)

Directions

1. Set your Instant Pot to sauté mode and add onion, celery, and carrot.
2. Sauté them for about 3 minutes
3. Add lentils, turnip, bay leaf, thyme, stock and rosemary.
4. Lock up the lid and let it cook at high pressure for 10 minutes.
5. Once done, release the pressure naturally.
6. Add flour to a dry skillet over medium-high heat to brown it.
7. Transfer to a bowl once the flour is toasted.
8. Add 1 tablespoon of browned flour alongside the Worcestershire sauce tomatoes.
9. Lock up it again and let it cook for another 3 minutes.
10. Quick release the pressure by switching the pressure valve to "venting".
11. Toss away the bay leaf and transfer the whole mix into a casserole dish or 4 ramekins.
12. Top it up with some mashed potatoes and brown them in your oven. Serve!

Cinnamon Swirl French Toast with Vanilla

(Total Time: 25 Min|Serves: 2)

Ingredients

- 1 ½ cups Water
- 1 tsp Butter
- 1 ½ cups Cinnamon Swirl Bread Cubes
- 1 tbsp Maple Syrup
- ½ tsp Vanilla Extract
- 2 Medium Eggs
- 1/2 cup Milk
- ½ tsp Sugar
- Pinch of Salt

Directions

1. Pour the water into the Instant Pot. Lower the rack.
2. Grease a small baking dish with the butter.

3. Place the cinnamon swirl bread cubes inside.
4. Whisk together the remaining ingredients in a bowl.
5. Pour the mixture over the bread.
6. Close the lid and select MANUAL.
7. Cook on HIGH for 15 minutes.
8. Do a quick pressure release by switching the pressure valve to "venting".
9. Serve and enjoy!

Creamy Banana Bread Oatmeal
(Total Time: 2 Min|Serves: 2)

Ingredients

- ¼ cup chopped Walnuts
- 1 cup Oatmeal
- 1 Banana, mashed
- ½ tsp Vanilla
- 2 tbsp Honey
- 1 ¾ cup Water
- Pinch of Sea Salt

Directions

1. Place everything in your Instant Pot.
2. Give the mixture a good stir until fully incorporated.
3. Close the lid and choose the PORRIDGE cooking method.
4. Cook the oatmeal for 10 minutes.
5. Do a natural pressure release.
6. Serve and enjoy!

Cheese and Mushroom Thyme Oats

(Total Time: 30 Min|Serves: 2)

Ingredients

- 1 tbsp Butter
- ¼ Onion, diced
- 4 ounces Mushrooms, sliced
- 1 tsp minced Garlic
- ½ cup Steel-Cut Oats
- 7 ounces Chicken Broth
- ¼ cup Water
- 1 Thyme Sprigs
- ¼ cup grated Cheddar
- Pinch of Salt
- ¼ tsp Pepper

Directions

1. Melt the butter in your Instant Pot on SAUTE.
2. Add onions and mushrooms and cook for 3 minutes.
3. Stir in the garlic and cook for an additional minute.
4. Add the oats and cook for 30 seconds more.
5. Pour the broth and water and place the thyme inside.
6. Close the lid and cook for 12 minutes on PORRIDGE.
7. Release the pressure naturally and stir in the cheese, salt and pepper.
8. Serve and enjoy!

Extremely Elegant Simple Broccoli

(Total Time: 3Min|Serves: 2)

Ingredients

- ¾ cup of water
- 1 medium head broccoli
- Salt as needed
- Pepper as needed

Directions

1. Add ¾ cup of water to the pot
2. Chop up the broccoli into florets and place them on a steamer rack.
3. Place the rack on top of your pot.
4. Lock up the lid and cook on HIGH pressure for 2 minutes.

5. Once done, allow the pressure naturally.
6. Serve with a seasoning of salt and pepper.

A Potato Stew with Chard

(Total Time: 8Min|Serves: 2)

Ingredients

- 2 tablespoon of olive oil
- 1 teaspoon of cumin seed
- 1 medium sized diced up onion
- 1 jalapeno pepper
- ½ a teaspoon of turmeric
- 1 tablespoon of peeled minced fresh ginger
- 1 teaspoon of salt
- 2 medium sized sweet potatoes peeled up and cut into ½ inch cubes
- 1 teaspoon of ground coriander
- ¾ cup of water
- 1 bunch of Swiss chard
- 1 can of unsweetened coconut milk
- ¼ cup of finely chopped up fresh cilantro
- Lime wedges for serve

Directions

1. Set your pot to Sauté mode and add olive oil.
2. Allow the oil to heat up and add cumin seeds, wait until toasted.
3. After 3 minutes add onion, jalapeno, turmeric, ginger, salt, sweet potatoes and cook for 3 minutes more.
4. Add coriander and stir until you have a nice fragrance.
5. Pour water and a bit of salt alongside chard and coconut milk.
6. Lock up the lid and cook for 3 minutes at HIGH pressure
7. Perform a quick release by switching the pressure valve to "venting".
8. Garnish with a bit of lime and cilantro. Enjoy!

Tortellini Soup with Basil

(Total Time: 10Min|Serves: 3)

Ingredients

- 3 tablespoon of olive oil
- 1 large chopped up white onion
- 2 minced garlic cloves
- 1 medium sized coarsely cut carrot
- 1/8 teaspoon of red pepper flakes
- 6 cups of reduce chicken broth
- 1 can of tomato puree
- 1 can of diced up and undrained tomato
- 1 cup of minced fresh basil
- Salt as needed
- Ground black pepper

Directions

1. Set your pot to Sauté mode and grease the inner pot with olive oil.
2. Add the onion and let it cook for about 3 minutes.
3. Add in the garlic and keep stirring it for about 60 seconds.
4. Add in the carrot, pepper flakes and pour the broth.
5. Then stir in the tomato puree alongside the diced tomatoes with all of their juices and tortellini.
6. Close up your lid then and set the pressure to high and cook it at low temperature for 5 minutes.
7. Once done, wait for 10 minutes and release the pressure naturally.
8. Stir for a while tossing in some basil and let it stand for further 2 minutes.
9. Season with pepper and salt according to your desire and serve with a good assortment of grated cheese and rice on the side.
10. Drizzle with some olive oil

A Simple Bowl of Mushrooms

(Total Time: 30 Min|Serves: 8)

Ingredients

- 8 cups of beef stock/broth
- 1 pound of baby bella mushrooms sliced up

- 1 piece of diced medium onion
- 2 diced celery stalks
- 2 diced carrots
- 4 chopped up garlic cloves
- 4 sprigs of thyme
-
- 1 sprig of sage
- 1 teaspoon of salt
- ¼ teaspoon of fresh ground pepper
- ¼ teaspoon of garlic powder

Directions:

1. Add the ingredients to your pot and give it a nice stir.
2. Lock up the lid and cook for 20 minutes on HIGH pressure.
3. Release the pressure naturally over 10 minutes.
4. Remove the lid and stir well. Enjoy!

Early Morning Potato Soup

(Total Time: 20Min|Serves:4)

Ingredients

- 2 cups of Yukon Gold Potatoes
- 4 teaspoon of minced garlic cloves
- ½ a cup of diced onion
- 1 teaspoon of Season Salt
- 3 and a ¼ cup of chicken broth

Garnish

- 1/ cup of cooked and diced up bacon

Directions:

1. Add potatoes, garlic, onion, chicken stock and seasoning to the pot
2. Lock up the lid and cook for 10 minutes on SOUP setting.
3. Do a quick release by switching the pressure valve to "venting".
4. Set your pot to Sauté mode and stir for a while.
5. Garnish with some bacon and enjoy!

Bacon and Egg Sandwich

(Total Time: 22 Min|Serves: 2)

Ingredients

- 4 slices of Bacon
- 1 ½ cup Water
- 2 Eggs

- 2 tbsp grated Cheese
- 4 slices of Bread

Directions

1. Set your Instant Pot to SAUTE and add the bacon to it.
2. Cook until crispy. Transfer to a plate.
3. Pour the water into the IP and lower the rack.
4. Grease 2 ramekins and crumble the bacon in them.
5. Crack the eggs into the ramekins.
6. Top with grated cheese.
7. Place the ramekins on the rack and close the lid.
8. Cook on HIGH for 5 minutes.
9. Release the pressure and assemble the sandwiches.
10. Enjoy!

One Giant Coconut Pancake

(Total Time: 35 Min|Serves: 2)

Ingredients

- ¾ cup Coconut Milk
- 1 Egg
- 1 tbsp Honey
- ¼ tsp Baking Soda

- ¼ tsp Coconut Extract
- ½ cup Coconut Flour
- ½ up ground Almonds

Directions

1. Whisk together the coconut milk, egg, honey, baking soda, and coconut extract, in a bowl.
2. Stir in the remaining ingredients.

3. Grease your IP with cooking spray.
4. Pour the coconut batter into it.
5. Close the lid and set it to MANUAL.
6. Cook on LOW for 25 minutes.
7. Do a quick pressure release by switching the pressure valve to "venting".
8. Serve and enjoy!

Sweet Potato and Onion Frittata

(Total Time: 25 Min|Serves: 2)

Ingredients

- 1 ½ cups Water
- 1 tbsp Olive Oil
- 2 tbsp Milk
- 1 tbsp Tomato Paste
- 3 Eggs

- 1/4 Red Onion, diced
- 4 ounces shredded Sweet Potatoes
- 2 tbsp diced Tomatoes
- ¼ tsp Garlic Powder
- 1 tbsp Flour

Directions

1. Pour the water into the IP and lower the trivet.
2. Whisk together the oil, milk, tomato paste, and eggs, in a bowl.
3. In another bowl, combine the remaining ingredients.
4. Stir the wet mixture into the eggs.
5. Grease a baking dish and pour the mixture into it.
6. Place the baking dish inside the IP and close the lid.
7. Cook on HIGH for 15-18 minutes.
8. Do a quick pressure release by switching the pressure valve to "venting".
9. Serve and enjoy!

Heavenly Mana Chicken Stock

(Total Time: 80 Min|Serves: 4)

Ingredients

- 2 and a ½ pound of bones from pastured chicken
- 1 organic carrot (chopped up into thirds)
- 1 rib of celery chopped up into thirds
- 1 small sized shallot
- Green trimming from leek
- 1 piece of bay leaf
- ½ a teaspoon of whole black peppercorns
- 1 sprig of fresh parsley
- 1 teaspoon of kosher salt

Directions

1. Add chicken bones to the pot.
2. Rinse the veggies and herbs and add them to the bones.
3. Season with some pepper and salt.
4. Add water and fill the pot up to the "10" lining.
5. Lock up the cook under HIGH pressure for 10 minutes.
6. Release the pressure naturally over 10 minutes and remove the lid.
7. Strain the mix into a nice heat proof container.
8. Enjoy it immediately or allow it to chill and enjoy later!

Perfectly Marinated Seared Artichoke

(Total Time: 30Min|Serves: 4)

Ingredients

- 4 large pieces of artichokes
- 2 cups water
- 2 tablespoon of fresh lemon juice
- 2 teaspoon of balsamic vinegar
- ¼ up of olive oil
- 1 teaspoon of dried oregano
- 2 cloves of minced up garlic
- ½ a teaspoon of sea salt
- ¼ teaspoon of fresh ground black pepper

Directions

1. Rinse the artichokes and cut the stems off with a sharp knife.
2. Putt off the lower petals that are tough and small.
3. Cut off the upper inch of the artichoke.
4. Trim the thorny petals with a kitchen shears.

5. Place the chokes in the bottom of your inner pot and fitted with a steamer basket and pour 2 cups of water.
6. Choose the STEAM mode and reduce the cooking time to about 8 minutes.
7. In the meantime, prepare your marinade by placing the balsamic vinegar, lemon juice, oregano, olive oil, salt, pepper and garlic in a tiny jar.
8. Lock up the lid and shake it until well combined.
9. Once the steaming of the chokes is complete, let it cool and open up the lid.
10. Remove the center cone away from the prickly leaves and scrape away the thistle fuzz cover the choke heart.
11. Drizzle the marinade over your chokes and make sure to coat them finely letting to sit for 30 minutes. Serve.

French Toast with Bananas and Cinnamon

(Total Time: 30 Min|Serves: 2)

Ingredients

- 1 ½ cups Water
- 2 Bread Slices, cubed
- 2 Bananas, sliced
- 1 tbsp Cold Butter, sliced
- 1 tbsp Brown Sugar
- 2 tbsp Cream Cheese

- 2 tbsp chopped Pecans
- 2 eggs
- ¼ cup Milk
- 1 tsp Granulated Sugar
- 1 teaspoon vanilla extract
- ½ tsp Cinnamon

Directions

1. Pour the water into the IP and grease a baking dish with cooking spray.
2. Arrange ½ of the bread at the bottom of the dish.
3. Top with half of the banana sliced and sprinkle ½ of the brown sugar.
4. Spread the cream cheese over the sugary bananas.
5. Arrange the remaining bread and bananas.
6. Sprinkle the remaining brown sugar.
7. Top with pecans and butter.
8. Whisk together the eggs, milk, sugar, vanilla, and cinnamon.
9. Pour the egg mixture over the bread and bananas.

10.	Place the dish inside the IP and close the lid.

11. Cook on HIGH for 15-20 minutes.

12. Do a quick pressure release by switching the pressure valve to "venting".

13. Serve and enjoy!

Eggs and Mozzarella with Kale and Hollandaise Sauce

(Total Time: 12 Min|Serves: 2)

Ingredients

- 1 ½ cups Water
- 2 Bread Slices
- 1/3 cup chopped Kale

- 2 Eggs, whisked
- 2 Mozzarella Cheese Sliced
- 1 ounce Hollandaise Sauce

Directions

1.	Pour the water into the IP and lower the trivet.

2.	Grease 2 ramekins and place the bread slices, inside.

3.	Combine the kale and eggs and pour into the ramekins.

4.	Cover the ramekins with aluminum foil and place inside the IP.

5.	Cook for 5 minutes on HIGH.

6.	Release the pressure quickly by switching the pressure valve to "venting".

7.	Remove the foil and place the mozzarella on top.

8.	Drizzle with hollandaise sauce.

9.	Enjoy!

Very Healthy Green Zoodles

(Total Time: 27Min|Serves: 4)

Ingredients

- 1 and a ½ tablespoon of brown butter ghee
- ½ a cup of sliced carrots
- 2 cups of sliced leeks

- 4 pieces of garlic cloves
- 2 tablespoon of apple cider vinegar
- 1 teaspoon of Italian herb blend of rosemary, basil, thyme, oregano and sage
- 1 teaspoon of rosemary
- 1 and a ½ pound of boneless skinless chicken thigh
- ½ a cup of nutritional yeast
- 1 tablespoon of great lakes beef gelatin
- 2 large sized zucchini
- ½ a teaspoon of salt
- 1 cloves of garlic
- 1 bunch of broccoli rabe
- Fist full of greens such as arugula, spinach and baby kale
- Extra ghee

Directions

1. Set your pot to Sauté mode and add ghee and allow it to melt.
2. Add carrots, leeks, garlic to your pot.
3. Allow them to Sauté for a while add vinegar, followed by herbs, chicken, yeast and lastly beef gelatin. Stir well.
4. Set your pot to poultry setting and cook for about 25 minutes
5. Spiralize your zucchini into zoodles and season with some salt.
6. Cover them up with a towel and keep them on the side.
7. Dice up your broccoli and sauté them in a skillet over high heat with more ghee.
8. Stir well then turn off the heat and add the greens.
9. Mix well and season with some salt.
10. Once the chicken is done, release pressure naturally and remove the chicken.
11. Shred the chicken using fork and allow it to cool (the veggies in the pot as well).
12. Add the zoodles and the broccoli mix to a bowl.
13. Spoon the chicken over the veggies and serve altogether!

Fancy Spaghetti Squash With Duck Fat Glaze

(Total Time: 33Min|Serves: 4)

Ingredients

- 1 spaghetti squash of 3 pound
- ¾ cup of apple juice
- 2 tablespoon of duck fat
- Sea salt as needed

Directions

1. Place a steam insert on top of your pot and add 1 cup water.
2. Place the squash on top of the steamer insert.
3. Lock up the lid and cook on HIGH pressure for 20 minutes.
4. Once done, release the pressure naturally.
5. Remove the squash to your cutting board and cut it in half.
6. Allow it to cool.
7. Remove the rack and empty the water from your pot.
8. Set your pot to Sauté mode.
9. Pour apple juice to your pot and allow it cook for 3 minutes until it simmers.
10. Add duck fat and stir until the fat has melted.
11. Scoop out the seeds of your squash and discard them.
12. Scrap the squash noodles into your pot using a fork.
13. Season with some salt and toss well. Serve!

Maple and Vanilla Quinoa Bowl

(Total Time: 15 Min|Serves: 2)

Ingredients

- ½ cup Quinoa
- 1 tbsp Maple Syrup
- ½ tsp Vanilla Extract
- A pinch of Salt
- 1 ½ cups Water

Directions

1. Place everything in the Instant Pot.
2. Stir to combine the mixture well.
3. Close the lid and set the IP to MANUAL.
4. Cook on HIGH for 1 minute.
5. Let sit covered for 10 minutes, then release the pressure quickly.

6. Divide between bowls and serve.

7. Enjoy!

Cherry Dark Chocolate Oat Porridge

(Total Time: 15 Min|Serves: 2)

Ingredients

- ½ cup Steel-Cut Oats
- ½ cup pitted Frozen Cherries
- 1 ¾ cup Water
- 1 tsp Sugar
- Pinch of Salt
- 2 tbsp Dark Chocolate Chips

Directions

1. Place everything but the chocolate chips in the Instant Pot.
2. Stir to combine well.
3. Close and lock the lid and set the IP to PORRIDGE.
4. Cook for 12 minutes.
5. Do a quick pressure release by switching the pressure valve to "venting".
6. Stir in the dark chocolate chips immediately.
7. Serve and enjoy!

A Green Soup Worthy for Hulk

(Total Time: 120 Min|Serves: 4)

Ingredients

- 1 chopped up onion
- 4 chopped up garlic cloves
- 3 chunks of carrots
- 1 sweet potato cut into chunks
- 6 cups of water
- 8 ounce of halved mushrooms
- 2 pound of chopped greens (such as kale, Swiss Chard, bok Choy etc.)
- 2 teaspoon of oregano
- 1 teaspoon of celery salt
- 1 teaspoon of thyme
- ½ a teaspoon of freshly ground black pepper

- 3 tablespoon of nutritional yeast
- ½ a cup of finely chopped fresh basil
- 1 tablespoon of cashew butter
- 1 tablespoon of lemon juice
- Salt as needed
- Lemon Slice for garnish

Directions

1. Add the first 6 ingredients to the Instant Pot.
2. Lock up the pot and cook on HIGH pressure for 8 minutes.
3. Allow the pressure to release naturally.
4. Open the lid and blend using an immersion blender.
5. Add the next 6 ingredients and lock up again.
6. Cook over SOUP mode for 30-45 minutes.
7. Allow the pressure to release naturally.
8. Add the remaining ingredients and blend well until smooth.
9. Add a bit of water if the mixture seems to thick.
10. Serve with a bit of lemon juice. Enjoy!

The Fantastic Potato Gratin

(Total Time: 25 Min|Serves: 4)

Ingredients

- 3 tablespoon of olive oil
- 3 cups of sliced up parsnips
- 3 cloves of chopped up garlic
- 2 cups of vegetable broth
- 1 tablespoon of black pepper
- 1 tablespoon of garlic powder
- 1 cup of Whole30 Mayo

Directions

1. Set your pot to Sauté mode and add ingredients except mayo.
2. Lock up the lid and cook on HIGH pressure for 5 minutes.
3. Release the pressure naturally.
4. Open the lid and spread a bit of Whole30 mayo all over.
5. Set your pot to Sauté mode and warm for a while.
6. Enjoy!

Salsa Eggs

(Total Time: 25 Min|Serves: 2)

Ingredients

- 1 ½ cup Water
- ¾ cup Salsa
- 2 Eggs
- Pinch of Salt
- Pinch of Pepper
- 1 tbsp chopped Parsley

Directions

1. Grease 2 ramekins with some cooking spray.
2. Pour the water into the IP and lower the trivet.
3. Divide the salsa between the ramekins and crack the eggs into them.
4. Sprinkle with salt and pepper.
5. Cover the ramekins with foil and place inside the IP.
6. Close the lid and set to MANUAL.
7. Cook on LOW for 20 minutes.
8. Do a quick pressure release by switching the pressure valve to "venting".
9. Serve sprinkled with chopped parsley and enjoy!

Eggs with Ham and Gruyere

(Total Time: 10 Min|Serves: 2)

Ingredients

- 1 tsp Butter
- 2 Ham Slices
- 2 Eggs
- 2 Gruyere Cheese Slices
- 1 tsp chopped Dill

Directions

1. Grease two ramekins with the butter.
2. Place the ham slices inside.
3. Crack the eggs into the ramekins.
4. Top with a Gruyere slice.
5. Pour the water into the Instant Pot and lower the trivet.

6. Place the ramekins on the trivet and close the lid.
7. Set the IP to MANUAL and cook on HIGH for 4 minutes.
8. Release the pressure by switching the pressure valve to "venting".
9. Sprinkle with dill before serving.
10. Enjoy!

Jalapeno Hash with Bacon

(Total Time: 15 Min|Serves: 2)

Ingredients

- 2 tbsp Olive Oil, divided
- 1 ½ cups grated Sweet Potatoes
- 1 ½ cups Water
- ½ Onion, chopped
- 1 Jalapeno Pepper, chopped

- 2 Eggs
- 2 tbsp chopped Cilantro
- 2 Bacon Slices, cooked and crumbled
- Salt and Pepper, to taste

Directions

1. Grease a baking dish with half of the olive oil.
2. Place the grated sweet potatoes inside.
3. Pour the water into the IP and lower the lid.
4. Place the dish inside the IP and close the lid.
5. Cook on MANUAL for 2 minutes.
6. Do a quick pressure release and transfer to a bowl.
7. Discard the water from the IP and heat the remaining oil in it on SAUTE.
8. Add onions and cook until soft.
9. Add jalapeno and cook for 1 more minute.
10. Crack the eggs inside and scramble.
11. Cook until set then transfer the mixture to the bowl with potatoes.
12. Top with bacon and cilantro and serve.
13. Enjoy!

Feistily Pounded Carrot Puree

(Total Time: 15 Min|Serves: 6)

Ingredients

- 1 and a ½ pound of roughly chopped up carrots
- 1 tablespoon of clarified butter
- 1 tablespoon of date paste
- ¼ teaspoon of sea salt
- 1 cup of water

Directions

1. Pour 1 cup of water to the pot.
2. Place a steamer rack on top of the pot and add chopped carrots.
3. Lock up the lid and cook on HIGH pressure for 4 minutes.
4. Do a quick release by switching the pressure valve to "venting".
5. Remove the carrots and dry them.
6. Take a deep bowl and transfer the carrots.
7. Use an immersion blender to blend everything.
8. Add date paste, clarified butter, salt and stir. Enjoy!

A Generous Bowl of Carrot and Kale

(Total Time: 40 Min|Serves: 4)

Ingredients

- 1 tablespoon of nice ghee
- 1 medium sized thinly sliced onion
- 3 medium sized carrots cut into half inch pieces
- 5 cloves of peeled and chopped up garlic
- 10 ounces of roughly chopped up kale
- ½ a cup of chicken broth
- Kosher salt
- Freshly grounded pepper
- Vinegar
- ½ teaspoon of red pepper flakes

Directions

1. Set your pot to Sauté mode and add ghee, allow it to melt.
2. Add chopped up onion and carrot and sauté until tender.

3. Add garlic and keep cooking until a nice fragrance comes.
4. Add kale and pour chicken broth.
5. Sprinkle salt and pepper.
6. Lock up the lid and cook for 8 minutes at HIGH pressure.
7. Release the pressure naturally.
8. Open up the lid and give a swirl to make sure that everything is in order.
9. Pour down the vinegar and sprinkle some more pepper flakes, if desired.

Raisin Cheesecake Porridge

(Total Time: 20 Min|Serves: 2)

Ingredients

- 1 tbsp Butter
- ½ cup Oats
- 1 ¾ cups Water
- 2 tbsp Brown Sugar
- 1 tsp White Sugar
- Pinch of Sea Salt
- ½ tsp Cinnamon
- 1/3 cup Raisins
- 1 tsp Milk
- 2 tbsp Cream Cheese

Directions

1. Melt the butter inside the Instant Pot on SAUTE.
2. Add oats and cook for 2 minutes.
3. Add water, sugar, and salt.
4. Choose the PORRIDGE mode and cook for 10 minutes.
5. Do a natural pressure release.
6. Stir in the remaining ingredients.
7. Divide the between two bowls.
8. Serve and enjoy!

The Ultimate Pot of Rhubarb and Strawberry Compote

(Total Time: 20 Min|Serves: 4)

Ingredients

- 2 pounds of rhubarb
- ½ a cup of water
- 1 pound of strawberries
- 3 tablespoon of date paste
- Fresh mint

Directions

1. Peel the rhubarb using a paring knife and chop it up ½ inch pieces.
2. Add the chopped rhubarb to your pot with the water.
3. Lock up the lid and cook on HIGH pressure for 10 minutes.
4. Stem and quarter your strawberries and keep them on the side.
5. Add the strawberries and date paste, give it a nice stir.
6. Lock up the lid and cook on HIGH pressure for 20 minutes.
7. Release the pressure naturally and enjoy the compote!

Chapter 2: Lunch Recipes

Authentic Shredded Chicken

(Total Time: 24Min|Serves: 6)

Ingredients

- 4 pounds of chicken breast
- ½ a cup of chicken broth
- 1 teaspoon of salt
- ½ a teaspoon of black pepper

Directions

1. Add all of the ingredients into your pot.
2. Give it a stir and lock up the lid.
3. Cook for about 20 minutes at HIGH pressure.
4. Once ready, allow the pressure to release naturally over 10 minutes.

5. Take the chicken out and place it on a cutting board.
6. Shred it using fork.
7. Serve it immediately or store it in jars for later use. Enjoy

The "Squash" Spaghetti

(Total Time: 152Min|Serves: 4)

Ingredients

- 2 pound of spaghetti squash
- 1 cup of water

Directions

1. Take a paring knife and cut the spaghetti squash in half.
2. Take a large spoon and scoop out the seeds.
3. Place a steamer rack and place it over your pot.
4. Transfer the squash to the rack and add 1 cup of water to the pot.
5. Make sure that the cut parts of the halved squash are facing up.
6. Lock up the lid and cook on HIGH pressure for 7 minutes.
7. Quick release the pressure by switching the pressure valve to "venting".
8. Take the squash out and add a bit of sauce and your favorite topping.
9. Enjoy the Squash noodles!

Corned Beef with Potatoes and Red Cabbage

(Total Time: 90 Min|Serves: 2)

Ingredients

- ¾ pounds Corned Beef
- 1 ¾ cup Water
- Salt and Pepper, to taste
- 1/3 pounds Carrots, sliced

- 1 pound Red Cabbage, chopped
- ½ pounds Small Potatoes
- 1/2 Celery Stalk, chopped
- ¼ Onion, diced

Directions

1. Combine the beef and water in the IP and season with some salt and pepper.
2. Close the lid and choose MANUAL.
3. Cook on HIGH for 70 minutes.
4. Do a quick pressure release and transfer the beef to a plate.
5. Add the remaining ingredients to the water, close the lid, and cook on HIGH for 5 more minutes.
6. Transfer the veggies to the plate with the cooked beef.
7. Serve and enjoy!

Brown Sugar and Soy Short Ribs

(Total Time: 4 hours and 40 Min|Serves: 2)

Ingredients

- 2 Beef Short Ribs
- 6 tbsp Soy Sauce
- Juice of ½ Orange
- 1/4 tbsp Sesame Oil

- ½ tsp grated Ginger
- 2 tsp minced Garlic
- 1 cup Water

Directions

1. Combine all of the ingredients in a bowl.
2. Coat well and cover the bowl.
3. Place in the fridge and let marinate for 4 hours.
4. Transfer everything to your Instant Pot.
5. Close the lid and set it to MANUAL.
6. Cook on HIGH for 30 minutes.
7. Do a natural pressure release.
8. Enjoy!

Fine Fennel Shredded Chicken

(Total Time: 40Min|Serves: 6)

Ingredients

- ¼ cup of fennel bulb
- 4 garlic cloves
- 2 inch nub of fresh ginger
- 2 pound of skinless chicken thigh
- 3 tablespoon of bacon fat
- 3 tablespoon of full fat of coconut milk
- 1 tablespoon of apple cider vinegar
- 1 teaspoon of cinnamon
- 2 teaspoon of turmeric
- 1 and a ½ teaspoon of salt
- 1 teaspoon of dried basil leaves
- Sprigs of parsley

Directions

1. Prepare your vegetables by dicing the fennel, peeling and dicing the garlic, and peeling the ginger.
2. Add the chicken to your pot.
3. Add bacon fat, coconut milk, vinegar, and seasoning to the pot.
4. Add fennel, garlic and ginger to the pot and toss well.
5. Lock up the lid and allow it to cook for about 29 minutes under poultry mode.
6. Once done, allow the pressure to release naturally.
7. Set the pot to Sauté mode and keep for 10 minutes, allow it to reduce the juices.
8. Once it comes to a boil, stir twice.
9. Once the reducing is done, shred the chicken using two forks.
10. Serve with garnish of fennel greens. Have fun!

A Chicken "Faux" Pho

(Total Time: 50Min|Serves: 4)

Ingredients

- 1 tablespoon of coriander seed
- 4 pound of chicken bone-in chicken pieces

- 2 medium sized quartered onions
- 1 inch roughly chopped and peeled ginger
- 1 black cardamom pod
- 1 cinnamon stick
- 4 pieces of clove
- 1 lemon grass stalk cut up into 2 inch pieces
- ¼ cup of fish sauce
- 1 cup of fresh cilantro
- 1 head of roughly chopped Bok Choy
- 1 large sized spiralized daikon root
- Sea salt as needed

For garnish

- Lime wedges
- Fresh basil
- Thinly sliced jalapenos
- ¼ of an onion, thinly sliced

Directions

1. Place a skillet over medium-low heat and add coriander seed.
2. Toast them for about 5-6 minutes.
3. Rinse the chicken pieces well and add them to your pot.
4. Add dry spices, onion, lemon grass, cilantro, fish sauce.
5. Pour cold water to cover them up.
6. Lock up the lid and allow it to cook for about 30 minutes over HIGH pressure.
7. Once done, release the pressure naturally.
8. Remove the chicken and shred them.
9. Strain the broth and add it back to your pot – season with salt.
10. Bring it to a simmer and add Bok Choy and Spiralized Daikon.
11. Cook for about 5-6 minutes.
12. Divide the noodle and shredded chicken into serving bowls and ladle the broth in Garnish with your preferred ingredients and enjoy!

Spicy Shrimp and Tomato Casserole

(Total Time: 30 Min|Serves: 2)

Ingredients

- 1 tbsp Olive Oil
- ¼ Onion, diced
- ½ tsp minced Garlic
- ¾ pound Tomatoes, chopped

- 2 tbsp chopped Cilantro
- ¼ cup Clam Juice
- 1 tbsp Lime Juice
- ¾ pound Shrimp, peeled and deveined
- ½ Jalapeno, diced
- ½ cup shredded Cheddar Cheese

Directions

1. Set the IP to SAUTE.
2. Heat the oil and sauté the onions for 3 minutes.
3. Add garlic and cook for one more minute.
4. Add tomatoes, cilantro, and pour the clam juice and lime juice over.
5. Close the lid and cook on HIGH for 8 minutes.
6. Do a quick pressure release and stir in the shrimp.
7. Cook for 2 more minutes.
8. Release the pressure quickly and top with the cheese and jalapeno.
9. Serve and enjoy!

Turkey with Cranberries and Sauerkraut

(Total Time: 35 Min|Serves: 2)

Ingredients

- ¾ cup Sauerkraut
- 1 tbsp Raisins
- 1 tsp minced Garlic
- Juice of ½ Lemon
- ½ cup Cranberries
- 2 Turkey Thighs
- ½ tsp Salt
- 1/3 cup Apple Cider
- ½ tsp Red Pepper Flakes
- 1 tsp Flour

Directions

1. Place the sauerkraut in the IP.
2. Top with raisins, garlic, lemon juice and half of the cranberries.
3. Add the turkey on top and sprinkle with salt.
4. Cook on HIGH for 25 minutes.
5. Transfer the meat to a plate.
6. Set the IP to Sauté and whisk in the flour.

7. Cook for 2 minutes.
8. Release the pressure quickly by switching the pressure valve to "venting".
9. Stir in the remaining cranberries.
10. Pour the mixture over the thighs.
11. Serve and enjoy!

Lettuce Wrap "Taco" Chicken

(Total Time: 15 Min|Serves: 5)

Ingredients

- 2 pounds of boneless and skinless chicken breast
- 1 teaspoon of chili powder + ½ a teaspoon of kosher salt
- 1 cup of roasted tomato salsa
- Grain free tortillas/ lettuce wraps

Directions

1. Arrange your chicken in a single layer in your cooker pot.
2. Season the chicken with salt on both sides.
3. Pour salsa evenly on top of your chicken pieces.
4. Lock up the lid and allow it to cook for about 7 minutes over HIGH pressure.
5. Once done, release the pressure quickly by switching the pressure valve to "venting".
6. Remove the lid and transfer the chicken to a bowl.
7. Shred it up using fork.
8. Serve the chicken by adding them to your tortilla or lettuce wraps
9. Enjoy!

Mexican Rice Casserole

(Total Time: 35 Min|Serves: 2)

Ingredients

- ½ cup Black Beans, soaked overnight and drained
- 2 ½ cups Water
- 3 ounces Tomato Paste
- 1 tsp Chili Powder
- ½ tsp minced Garlic
- 1 cup Brown Rice
- 1 tsp Onion Powder

Directions

1. Combine everything in the Instant Pot.
2. Close the id and set it to MANUAL.
3. Cook on HIGH for 25 minutes.
4. Do a quick pressure release by switching the pressure valve to "venting".
5. Serve and enjoy!

Pasta Bolognese

(Total Time: 12 Min|Serves: 2)

Ingredients

- 1 tbsp Olive Oil
- ¾ pounds ground Beef
- 1 clove minced garlic
- 6 ounces Water
- 4 ounces dried Pasta
- ½ tsp Italian Seasoning
- 12 ounces Pasta Sauce

Directions

1. Set your Instant Pot to SAUTE and heat the olive oil in it.
2. Add the beef and cook until brown.
3. Add garlic and cook for one more minute.
4. Stir in all of the remaining ingredients.
5. Close the lid and choose MANUAL.
6. Cook on HIGH for 5 minutes.
7. Release the pressure quickly by switching the pressure valve to "venting".
8. Serve and enjoy!

Heartwarming Spaghetti Squash and Chicken Marsala

(Total Time: 30Min|Serves: 5)

Ingredients

- 1 cup water
- 1 large spaghetti squash
- 1 teaspoon of coconut oil
- 2 pound of boneless chicken breast
- Salt as needed
- Pepper as needed

- 2 cloves of minced garlic
- 1 cup of Marsala cooking wine
- 1 cup of sliced shitake mushrooms
- ½ a cup of organic chicken broth
- 3 tablespoons of unflavored gelatin
- Fresh basil

Directions

1. Place the steamer rack on top of your pot.
2. Add 1 cup of water and add the spaghetti squash to the rack.
3. Seal up the lid and allow it to cook on high pressure for 20 minutes.
4. Allow it to release the pressure naturally.
5. Discard the water and allow the pot to dry.
6. Set the pot to Sauté mode and add coconut oil.
7. Add chicken, salt, and pepper then sear until browned.
8. Top with garlic, Marsala, and mushrooms.
9. Lock up the lid and cook for about 7-8 minutes on HIGH pressure.
10. Release the pressure naturally.
11. Stir the chicken broth into the pot and allow it to warm.
12. Remove ¼ cup of the liquid and add the gelatin.
13. Once dissolved, add the slurry back to the pot and mix well.
14. Cut up your squash in half and scoop out the seeds.
15. Separate the squash from the rind.
16. Arrange the noodles on your plate and top it up with chicken, Marsala sauce and mushrooms.
17. Garnish with a bit of fresh basil.
18. Enjoy!

Flavorful Bone Broth

(Total Time: 125 Min|Serves: 5)

Ingredients

- 2 medium sized leeks cleaned and cut up half crosswise
- 1 medium sized carrots peeled up and cut up into 3 pieces
- 2 and a half pound of assorted bones (chicken and pork bones)
- 8 cups of water
- 1 teaspoon of apple cider vinegar
- 2 tablespoons of Red Boat Fish Sauce

Directions

1. Add the vegetables and bones to your cooker and enough water to submerge them.
2. Add vinegar and fish sauce.
3. Lock up the lid and cook on HIGH pressure for 120 minutes.
4. Release the pressure naturally.
5. Open and skim any scum. Strain the broth and serve!

Supremely Spicy And Ravaging Chicken Stew

(Total Time: 30 Min|Serves: 4)

Ingredients

- 1 and a ½ pound of boneless skinless chicken thigh
- 1 can of fire roasted crushed tomatoes
- 1 thinly sliced bell pepper
- 1 thinly sliced onion
- 3 minced garlic cloves
- 2 cups of bone broth
- ½ a cup of water
- 1 tablespoon of cumin
-]1 tablespoon of chili powder
- 1 teaspoon of oregano
- ½ a teaspoon of smoked paprika
- ½ a teaspoon of sea salt
- ½ a teaspoon of ground pepper

Directions

1. Add the ingredients to your pot except garnish and lock up the lid.

2. Allow them to cook under HIGH pressure for 20 minutes.
3. Release the pressure naturally.
4. Shred the chicken using fork and ladle the soup to serving bowl.
5. Enjoy by garnishing with a bit of fresh cilantro.

Thyme and Rosemary Lambs with Carrots

(Total Time: 35 Min|Serves: 2)

Ingredients

- 1 tbsp Olive Oil
- ¾ pounds Lamb, cubed
- 1 ½ cups Chicken Stock
- 3 tbsp Flour
- ½ cup sliced Carrots

- 1 tsp minced Garlic
- 1 Rosemary Sprig
- 1 Thyme Sprig
- Salt and Pepper, to taste

Directions

1. Heat the oil in your Instant Pot on Sauté mode.
2. Add lamb and cook until browned on all sides.
3. In a small bowl, whisk the stock and flour.
4. Pour the mixture over the lamb.
5. Stir in the remaining ingredients and close the lid.
6. Cook on HIGH for 20 minutes.
7. Do a quick release by switching the pressure valve to "venting". Serve.

Chili Chicken Curry

(Total Time: 35 Min|Serves: 2)

Ingredients

- ½ can Corn, undrained
- 1 tsp Cumin
- 1 tsp Chili Powder

- ½ pound Chicken Breasts, cut into cubes
- ½ can chopped Tomatoes
- ½ tbsp Curry Powder

- 1 ¼ cup Chicken Broth

Directions

1. Place all of the ingredients in the Instant Pot.
2. Give it a good stir and close the lid.
3. Cook the curry on HIGH for 20 minutes.
4. Let the pressure drop naturally.
5. Serve immediately and enjoy!

Beef and Mushroom Stew

(Total Time: 30 Min|Serves: 2)

Ingredients

- 1 tbsp Canola Oil
- ½ Onion, chopped
- ¾ pound Beef, chopped
- 2 carrots, sliced
- 2 potatoes, cut into chunks
- 1 cup sliced Mushrooms
- 5 ounces Golden Mushroom Soup
- 6 ounces Water
- ½ tsp dried Parsley

Directions

1. Heat the oil in the IP on SAUTE.
2. Add onion and cook for 2 minutes.
3. Add beef and cook until it becomes brown on all sides.
4. Add the remaining ingredients and give it a good stir.
5. Close the lid and choose MANUAL.
6. Cook on HIGH for 15 minutes.
7. Do a natural pressure release.
8. Serve and enjoy!

Blessed Ligurian Chicken

(Total Time: 25 Min|Serves: 4)

Ingredients

- 2 chopped up garlic cloves
- ½ a bunch of parsley
- 2 sprigs of fresh sage
- 3 sprigs of fresh rosemary
- 3 pieces of lemon completely juiced
- 4 tablespoon of extra virgin olive oil
- 1 teaspoon of sea salt
- ¼ a teaspoon of pepper
- 1 and ½ cup of water
- 1 whole piece of chicken, preferably cut into parts
- 3.50ounce of black gourmet salt-cured olives
- 1 fresh lemon

Directions

1. Take a bowl and add chopped garlic, parsley, sage and rosemary.
2. Pour lemon juice and olive oil into the bowl and season with salt and pepper.
3. Remove the chicken skin and from the chicken pieces and carefully transfer them to a dish.
4. Pour the marinade on top of the chicken pieces and chill for 2-4 hours.
5. Set your pot to Sauté mode and add olive oil, allow it to heat up.
6. Add chicken and browned on all sides.
7. Measure out the marinade and add to the pot (it should cover the chicken, add a bit of water if needed).
8. Lock up the lid and cook on HIGH pressure for 10 minutes.
9. Release the pressure naturally.
10. The chicken out and transfer to a platter then cover with foil and let cool.
11. Set your pot in Sauté mode and reduce the liquid to 1/4.
12. Add the chicken pieces again to the pot and allow them to warm.
13. Sprinkle a bit of olives, lemon slices and rosemary. Enjoy!

Amazing Beef Short Ribs

(Total Time: 25 Min|Serves: 5)

Ingredients

- 4 pound of beef short ribs
- Generous amount of Kosher Salt
- 1 tablespoon of beef fat
- 1 quartered onion with its skin on
- 3 cloves of garlic
- Water

Directions:

1. Season the beef ribs well with salt by rubbing it all over.
2. Take a skillet and place it over medium heat.
3. Add oil and allow the oil to heat up.
4. Add ribs and cook until they are fully browned up.
5. Add garlic, onion and fill it up with water (just up to below 2 inch of its height).
6. Give it a nice mix and transfer the mixture to the pot.
7. Lock up the lid and cook on HIGH pressure for 35 minutes.
8. Release the pressure naturally over 10 minutes.
9. Serve and enjoy!

Instant Halved Chicken

(Total Time: 30 Min|Serves: 2)

Ingredients

- 1 half of a 2-pound Chicken
- ¼ tsp Salt
- Pinch of Pepper
- ¼ tsp Garlic Powder
- ¼ tsp Thyme
- 1 ½ cups Water
- 1 tbsp Olive Oil

Directions

1. Season the chicken with the thyme and spices.
2. Heat the oil in the IP on SAUTE.
3. Add the chicken and cook it until brown on all sides.
4. Pour the water around the chicken.
5. Close the lid and choose MANUAL.
6. Cook for 20 minutes on HIGH.
7. Release the pressure quickly by switching the pressure valve to "venting".

8. Serve and enjoy!

Fish and Potatoes Packet

(Total Time: 15 Min|Serves: 2)

Ingredients

- 2 Fish Fillets
- 2 Thyme Sprigs
- 1 Potato, sliced
- ¼ Onion, sliced

- 2 tsp chopped Fresh Parsley
- ½ Lemon, sliced
- 1 tbsp Olive Oil
- 1 ½ cups Water

Directions

1. Place each of the fillets on top of a piece of parchment paper.
2. Top with the remaining ingredients, except the water.
3. Wrap the fillets firmly.
4. Then, take the wrapped fish and place on a piece of aluminum foil. Wrap again.
5. Pour the water into the IP.
6. Lower the trivet and place the wrapped fillets on top of it.
7. Close the lid and cook on HIGH for 5 minutes.
8. Do a quick release by switching the pressure valve to "venting". Serve.

Kale and Spinach Risotto

(Total Time: 30 Min|Serves: 2)

Ingredients

- 2 tsp Olive oil
- 2 tbsp diced Onion
- ¾ cup Arborio Rice
- 1 ¾ cups Water
- ½ cup Spinach

- ½ cup Kale
- 3 tbsp grated Parmesan Cheese
- 2 Sun-Dried Tomatoes, chopped
- Salt and Pepper, to taste

Directions

1. Heat the oil in your IP.
2. Add the onions and cook for a few minutes, until soft.
3. Add the rice and cook for 2 minutes.
4. Add the water, stir to combine, and close the lid.
5. Cook for 6 minutes on RICE.
6. Release the pressure quickly by switching the pressure valve to "venting".
7. Stir in the remaining ingredients and let sit for a minute or two before serving.
8. Enjoy!

Thick Pork Chops With Artichoke and Lemon
(Total Time: 29 Min|Serves: 4)

Ingredients

- 2 tablespoons of clarified butter
- 3 ounces of pancetta diced of chunks
- 2 pieces of 2-inch thick bone-in pork loin or rib chops
- 2 teaspoon of ground black pepper
- 1 medium sized minced shallots
- 4 pieces of 2-inch lemon zest strips
- 1 teaspoon of dried rosemary
- 2 teaspoons of minced garlic
- 1 piece of 9-ounce box of frozen artichoke heart quarters
- ¼ cup of chicken broth

Directions:

1. Set your pot to Sauté mode and add butter and pancetta, cook for 5 minutes.
2. Transfer the browned pancetta to a plate and season your chops with pepper.
3. Add the chops to your pot and cook for 4 minutes.
4. Transfer the chops to a plate and keep repeating until they all of them are browned.
5. Add shallots to the pot and cook for 1 minute.
6. Add lemon zest, garlic, rosemary and garlic and stir until aromatic
7. After a while, stir in broth and artichokes.
8. Return the pancetta back to the cooker with the chops.
9. Lock up the lid and let it cook for about 24 minutes at HIGH pressure.
10. Release pressure quickly by switching the pressure valve to "venting".
11. Unlock and transfer the chops to a carving board.

12. Slice up the eye of your meat off the bone and slice the meat into strips.
13. Divide in serving bowls and sauce ladled up.

Mexican Chicken Cacciatore

(Total Time: 15 Min|Serves: 4)

Ingredients

- Extra virgin olive oil
- 3 chopped up shallots
- 1 seeded and sliced green bell pepper
- ½ a cup of organic chicken broth
- 4 crushed garlic cloves
- 10 ounce of sliced mushroom
- 5-6 pieces of skinless chicken breast

- 2 cans of organic crushed tomatoes
- 2 tablespoon of Organic Tomato Paste
- 1 can of pitted black olive
- Some fresh parsley
- Red pepper as required
- Salt as required
- Black pepper as required

Directions:

1. Pour the oil into the pot and start heating it on the Sauté setting.
2. Toss in the shallots, bell pepper and cook over medium heat for 2 minutes.
3. Pour down the broth and let it boil for about 2-3 minutes.
4. Toss in the garlic and mushroom with chicken on the top.
5. Gently cover up the chicken with the crushed tomatoes and tomato paste.
6. Close up the lid.
7. Bring the cooker to a high pressure and let it cook for about 8 minutes.
8. Once done, turn down the heat and release the pressure naturally.
9. Stir in some parsley, olive, salt, pepper and red pepper flakes. Serve hot!

Lobster and Cheese Pasta

(Total Time: 25 Min|Serves: 2)

Ingredients

- 3 cups Water

- 2 Lobster Tails

- 4 ounces Ziti
- 1 tbsp Flour
- ½ cup Heavy Cream
- ½ tbsp chopped Tarragon
- ½ cup grated Cheese
- ¼ cup White Wine
- ½ tbsp Worcestershire Sauce
- Salt and Pepper, to taste

Directions

1. Combine the water, lobster tails, and ziti in your IP.
2. Close the lid and cook on HIGH for 8 minutes.
3. Release the pressure quickly by switching the pressure valve to "venting".
4. Drain and transfer to a bowl.
5. Remove the meat from the lobster tails and place it in the pasta bowl.
6. Stir in the remaining ingredients.
7. Return back to the IP and cook on SAUTE for a few more minutes, or until thickened.
8. Serve and enjoy!

Juicy and Tender Chicken Drumsticks

(Total Time: 45 Min|Serves: 2)

Ingredients

- 1 tbsp Olive Oil
- ½ Onion diced
- 1 tsp minced Garlic
- 2 tbsp Tomato Paste
- 4 small Chicken Drumsticks
- 2 cups Water
- ¼ tsp Salt
- ¼ tsp Pepper

Directions

1. Heat the oil in your Instant Pot on SAUTE.
2. Add onion and garlic and cook for a few minutes.
3. Stir in the tomato paste and pour the water over.
4. Arrange the chicken drumsticks inside and close the lid.
5. Cook for 15 minutes on HIGH.
6. Do a natural pressure release.
7. Serve and enjoy!

Caribbean Beef

(Total Time: 45 Min | Serves: 2)

Ingredients

- 1 pound Beef Roast
- ½ tsp grated Ginger
- 2 Whole Cloves
- ½ tsp Thyme
- ¼ tsp Garlic Powder
- ¼ tsp Salt
- ½ tsp Turmeric
- 1 cup Water

Directions

1. Combine all of the herbs and spices in a small bowl and rub into the beef.
2. Stick the cloves into the meat.
3. Place the beef into the Instant Pot.
4. Pour the water around it and close the lid.
5. Cook on HIGH for 35 minutes.
6. Release the pressure quickly by switching the pressure valve to "venting".
7. Shred the meat with two forks inside the IP.
8. Stir to combine. Serve and enjoy!

Broccoli Soup with The Blessing Of The Divine

(Total Time: 10 Min | Serves: 4)

Ingredients

- 2 tablespoons of ghee
- The white parts of 3 medium sized leeks
- 2 roughly chopped medium sized shallots
- 1 tablespoon of Indian curry powder
- Kosher salt
- 1 and a 12 pound of chopped up broccoli
- ¼ cup of peeled up and diced apple
- 4 cups of chicken stock
- Freshly ground black pepper
- 1 cup of full fat coconut milk

Directions:

1. Set your pot to Sauté mode and melt the ghee.
2. Add vegetables (shallots, leeks etc.) and sauté them.
3. Add curry powder and sprinkle some salt.
4. Stir well until a nice fragrance comes.
5. Add chopped up broccoli and apple then stir well.
6. Pour chicken broth and submerge the veggies.
7. Cover up and cook for 5 minutes at HIGH pressure.
8. Allow the pressure to release naturally.
9. Once done, open the lid and blende the mixture using an immersion blender.
10. Pour coconut milk and season with some pepper and salt.
11. Blend again. Enjoy!

Amazing Pork Chop Of Ghee

(Total Time: 20 Min|Serves: 4)

Ingredients

- 2 tablespoons of ghee
- 4 pieces of ½ inch t hick bone-in pork loin or rib chops
- ½ a teaspoon of salt
- ½ teaspoon of ground black pepper
- 16 baby carrots
- 1 tablespoon of minced fresh dill fronds
- ½ a cup of white grape juice
- ½ a cup of chicken broth

Directions:

1. Set your pot to Sauté mode.
2. Season the pork chops well with salt and pepper.
3. Add the chops to your pot and cook for about 4 minutes.
4. Transfer the cooked chops (if any chops are left, repeat the Directions: with them as well. Bigger chops might require you to cook in batches).
5. Pour 1 tablespoon of ghee to the pot and add carrots, dill and cook for 1 minute.
6. Add ½ a cup of grape juice and deglaze the pot.
7. Stir in broth and return the chops to the cooker.
8. Lock up the lid and cook on HIGH pressure for about 18 minutes.

9. Do a natural release serve by pouring the cooking sauce on top. Enjoy!

Tender Soft Daikon Noodles
(Total Time: 25 Min|Serves: 2)

Ingredients

- 2 tablespoon of coconut oil
- 1 pound of boneless and skinless chicken thigh
- 1 cup of diced celery
- 1 cup of diced carrots
- ¾ cup of chopped green onion
- 6 cups of chicken stock
- ½ a teaspoon of dried basil
- 1 teaspoon of sea salt
- 1/6 teaspoon of fresh ground pepper
- 2 cups of Spiralized daikon noodles

Directions:

1. Set your pot to Sauté mode and add coconut oil.
2. Allow the oil to heat up and add the chicken thighs.
3. sauté for about 10 minutes.
4. Take the chicken out and shred it up.
5. Add celery, carrots, and onion to the pot and cook for 2 minutes more.
6. Add the rest of the ingredients and lock up the lid.
7. Cook on HIGH pressure for 15 minutes and quick release the pressure by switching the pressure valve to "venting".
8. Transfer the shredded chicken back to the noodle and stir. Enjoy!

Beef Tips in Sauce with Rice
(Total Time: 40 Min|Serves: 2)

Ingredients

- 1 pounds Sirloin Steak, cut into strips
- 1 ½ tbsp Flour
- ¼ tsp Paprika
- ¼ tsp Pepper
- 1 tbsp Oil
- 1 tsp minced Garlic

- 1 Onion, chopped
- 2 cups cooked Rice
- 10 ounces Beef Consomme

Directions

1. Place the steak, flour, paprika, and pepper, in a bowl.
2. Mix to coat well.
3. Heat the oil in your IP on SAUTE and cook the beef until browned on all sides.
4. Add garlic and onions and cook for 2 minutes.
5. Stir in the consommé and close.
6. Cook on HIGH for 20 minutes.
7. Do a quick pressure release by switching the pressure valve to "venting".
8. Stir in the rice. Serve and enjoy!

Tomato Tuna Pasta with Capers

(Total Time: 10 Min | Serves: 2)

Ingredients

- 1 tbsp Olive Oil
- 1 Garlic Clove, minced
- 14 ounces canned diced Tomatoes
- 1 ½ tbsp Capers
- 2 cups cooked Pasta
- 2 cans of Tuna, drained

Directions

1. Heat the oil in the IP on SAUTE.
2. Add garlic and cook for one minute or until it becomes fragrant.
3. Place everything else in the IP.
4. Stir to combine well and close the lid.
5. Set the Instant Pot to MANUAL.
6. Cook on HIGH for 1-2 minutes.
7. Do a quick pressure release by switching the pressure valve to "venting".
8. Serve topped with cheese if desired.
9. Enjoy!

The Very Curious Zuppa Toscana

(Total Time: 70 Min|Serves: 10)

Ingredients

- 2 tablespoon of olive oil
- 1 medium sized chopped yellow onion
- 3 minced garlic cloves
- 1 pound of Italian Sausage
- 3 large russet potatoes cut up into 1-inch chunks
- 5 cups of chicken broth
- 2 teaspoons of dried basil
- 1 teaspoon of dried fennel
- 2 cups of chopped fresh kale
- ½ a cup of full fat coconut milk
- 1 tablespoon of crushed red pepper
- Salt as needed
- Pepper as needed

Directions

1. Set your pot to Sauté mode and add oil.
2. Allow the oil to heat up and add chopped up onion.
3. Sauté for 2-3 minutes then add garlic and sausage.
4. Brown them for 5 minutes.
5. Pour chicken broth on top and add potatoes and herbs.
6. Lock up the lid and cook for 12 minutes at HIGH pressure.
7. Do a quick release by switching the pressure valve to "venting".
8. Stir in coconut milk and season with a bit of pepper and salt. Stir and enjoy!

Very Yummy Chicken Yum Yum (Whole30)

(Total Time: 45Min|Serves: 6)

Ingredients

- 2 pound of fresh boneless chicken thigh
- 3 tablespoon of homemade ketchup
- 1 and a ½ teaspoon of salt
- 2 teaspoon of garlic powder
- ¼ cup of ghee
- ½ teaspoon of finely ground black pepper
- 3 tablespoon of gluten free organic tamari

- ¼ cup of date paste

Directions:

1. Add all of the ingredients to your pot.
2. Stir well and make sure that the chicken is coated well.
3. Lock up the lid and cook on HIGH pressure for 18 minutes.
4. Once done, do a quick release by switching the pressure valve to "venting".
5. Transfer the chicken to a cutting board and shred it up.
6. Set your pot in Sauté mode and sauté for 5 minutes until the juice has been reduced.
7. Pour the sauce over your chicken and serve!

The Authentic Roast and Veggies

(Total Time: 145 Min|Serves: 6)

Ingredients

- 2 tablespoon of ghee
- 3 pounds of boneless chuck roast
- ½ a teaspoon of kosher salt
- ¼ a teaspoon of black pepper
- 1 small sized chopped up onion
- 1 minced garlic clove
- 1 tablespoon of tomato paste
- 1 cup of beef broth
- 1 cup of chicken broth
- 1 teaspoon of Worcestershire sauce
- 1 pound of carrot
- 8 ounces of white mushroom
- Salt as required
- Pepper as required

Directions:

1. Set your instant pot to Sauté mode
2. Add in the ghee and let it melt.
3. Add in the roast and let it brown on all sides for about 6 minutes total.
4. Once browned, remove the roast and add in the onions and sauté until they are softened, about 4 minutes.
5. Add in the garlic and pour the tomato paste.
6. After 30 seconds pour the broth and Worcestershire sauce and stir until simmer.

7. Add in the roast again and close the lid.

8. Cook for about 45 minutes at HIGH pressure.

9. Once done, quick release the pressure by switching the pressure valve to "venting".

10. Open up the lid and transfer the roast to a baking sheet aside.

11. Add in the carrots and mushroom and cook at HIGH pressure for 6 minutes in Stew/Meat mode.

12. Place the roast in the oven and broil it until the topside is crispy, about 4 minutes.

13. Remove the roast and transfer it a cutting board and cover to keep warm.

14. Transfer the vegies from the pot to the baking sheet.

15. Keep the pot in sauté mode and let it reduce the liquid by simmering it.

16. Place the veggies in oven until a nice broil for brown texture

17. Take a platter and slice up the roast and serve with the vegetables.

Goose with Apples and Raisins

(Total Time: 25 Min|Serves: 2)

Ingredients

- 1 tbsp Butter
- ¾ pounds boneless Goose, chopped
- 1 Apple, sliced
- ½ Shallot, chopped
- ¼ cup Raisins
- ½ tsp Dill
- 1 cup Chicken Broth

Directions

1. Melt the butter in the Instant Pot on SAUTE.

2. Add goose and cook until it becomes golden on all sides.

3. Stir in the remaining ingredients.

4. Close the lid and set to MANUAL.

5. Cook on HIGH for 15 minutes.

6. Do a quick pressure release by switching the pressure valve to "venting".

7. Serve immediately and enjoy!

Buffalo Chicken and Potatoes

(Total Time: 25 Min|Serves: 2)

Ingredients

- 1 ½ tbsp Butter
- ½ Onion, diced
- ¾ pound Chicken Breasts, cubed
- ½ tsp Onion Powder
- ¼ tsp Garlic Salt
- ¼ tsp Pepper
- 3 tbsp Buffalo Sauce
- 8 ounces diced Potatoes
- ½ cup Chicken Broth

Directions

1. Melt the butter in the IP on SAUTE.
2. Cook the onion for 3 minutes.
3. Add chicken and spices and cook until the chicken is no longer pink.
4. Add the remaining ingredients and stir well to combine.
5. Close and lock the lid and set it to POULTRY.
6. Cook for 15 minutes.
7. Do a quick pressure release by switching the pressure valve to "venting".
8. Serve and enjoy!

Pulled Pork with Cranberries

(Total Time: 30 Min|Serves: 2)

Ingredients

- 1 cup Water
- ¼ cup Cranberries
- ½ Chipotle Pepper, diced
- ½ tbsp Tomato Paste
- 1 tbsp Molasses
- 1 tsp Liquid moke
- 1 tbsp Adobo Sauce
- ¼ cup Tomato Puree
- ¾ cup Pork Roast
- 1 tbsp Apple Cider Vinegar
- 2 tbsp Buffalo Sauce

Directions

1. Place the water and cranberries in the IP.

2. Close the lid and cook on HIGH for 4 minutes.
3. Add the remaining ingredients and stir well to combine.
4. Cook the meat on HIGH for 40 minutes.
5. Release the pressure quickly by switching the pressure valve to "venting".
6. Shred the pork with 2 forks.
7. Serve drizzled with the sauce and topped with cranberries. Enjoy!

Pork Chops with Apples

(Total Time: 40 Min|Serves: 2)

Ingredients

- 1 tbsp Olive Oil
- 2 Pork Chops
- 2 Apples, sliced
- ¼ tsp Cinnamon
- ¼ cup Brown Sugar
- ½ cup Water
- 2 tbsp Flour

Directions

1. Set the IP to SAUTE.
2. Add the oil and pork chops.
3. Cook until the pork turns brown on all sides. Transfer to a plate.
4. Add all of the remaining ingredients to the IP and stir to combine.
5. Return the pork and close the lid.
6. Cook on MANUAL for 10 minutes.
7. Let the pressure drop naturally.
8. Serve the pork chops with the saucy apples. Enjoy!

Pulled Apart Pork Carnitas

(Total Time: 67 Min|Serves: 6)

Ingredients

- 4 pound of pork roast
- 2 tablespoon of olive oil
- 1 head butter lettuce
- 2 grated carrot
- 2 wedge cut limes
- Water

For the Spice Mixture

- 1 tablespoon of cocoa powder
- 1 tablespoon of salt
- 1 tablespoon of red pepper flakes
- 2 teaspoon oregano
- 1 teaspoon of white pepper
- 1 teaspoon of garlic powder
- 1 teaspoon of cumin
- 1/8 teaspoon of coriander
- 1/8 teaspoon of cayenne pepper
- 1 large finely chopped up onion

Directions:

1. Take a bowl and add the ingredients listed under "Spice", mix them well.
2. Season the roast with the spice mixture and chill overnight.
3. Set your pot to Sauté mode and add olive oil, allow the oil to heat up.
4. Add meat and brown it well then add the water.
5. Lock up the lid and cook on HIGH pressure for 50-60 minutes.
6. Release the pressure naturally.
7. Take out the meat shred the flesh from the bones.
8. Set your pot to Sauté mode and reduce the liquid by simmering it.
9. Add the shredded pork meat to a pan over medium heat and stir fry them until slightly brown.
10. Add some olive oil and spices.
11. Serve the fried pork pieces with the sauce. Enjoy

Amazing Beef Bourguignon

(Total Time: 40Min|Serves: 4)

Ingredients

- 1 tablespoon of olive oil
- 1 pound of stewing steak
- ½ a pound of bacon
- 5 medium sized carrots
- 1 large peeled and sliced red onion
- 2 minced cloves of garlic
- 2 teaspoon of rock salt
- 2 tablespoons of fresh Thyme
- 2 tablespoons of fresh parsley
- 2 teaspoon of ground black pepper
- ½ a cup of beef broth

Directions:

1. Set your pot to Sauté mode and add 1 tablespoon of oil.
2. Once the oil is hot, add the beef in batches and brown them.
3. Slice up your cooked bacon in strips.
4. Add the strips to the beef (with onions) and sauté them until brown.
5. Add the remaining ingredients and stir.
6. Lock up the lid and cook on HIGH pressure for 30 minutes.
7. Allow the pressure to release naturally and enjoy!

Very Curious Vietnamese Bo Kho

(Total Time: 60 Min|Serves: 4)

Ingredients

- ½ a teaspoon of ghee
- 2 ½ pounds of grass-fed beef brisket
- 1 yellow onion peeled and diced
- 1 and a ½ teaspoon of curry powder
- 2 and a ½ tablespoon of peeled up fresh ginger
- 2 cups of drained and crushed, diced up tomatoes
- 3 tablespoons of red boat fish sauce
- 2 tablespoons of applesauce
- 1 large stalk of lemongrass with the loose leaves trimmed off and cut into 3-inch pieces while being bruised with a meat pounder
- 2 whole sized star anise
- 1 piece of bay leaf
- 1 cup of bone broth

Directions:

1. Set your pot to Sauté mode and add ghee.
2. Allow the ghee to melt, add your brisket and fry until browned.

3. Remove the brisket and add onion, sauté them for a while.
4. Add curry powder, seared beef, ginger, fish sauce, diced tomatoes and star anise.
5. Pour apple sauce into the mix and stir well.
6. Add bay leaf and lemon grass.
7. Pour broth and lock up the lid, cook on HIGH pressure for 35 minutes.
8. Release the pressure naturally.
9. Add carrots and cook for 7 minutes more at HIGH pressure.
10. Release the pressure naturally and enjoy!

Classic Mac and Cheese

(Total Time: 10 Min | Serves: 2)

Ingredients

- 1 cup Chicken Stock
- ½ cup Heavy Cream
- ¼ cup Milk
- 1 ¼ cups Elbow Macaroni
- ½ tbsp Butter
- ¼ tsp Pepper
- ¼ tsp Pepper
- ¾ cup shredded Pepper Jack

Directions

1. Place everything in the Instant Pot.
2. Stir well to combine everything.
3. Close the lid and set the pot to MANUAL.
4. Cook on HIGH for 7-8 minutes.
5. Do a quick pressure release by switching the pressure valve to "venting".
6. Serve and enjoy!

Lemony Salmon

(Total Time: 10 Min | Serves: 2)

Ingredients

- 1 ½ cups Water
- 2 Salmon Fillets

- ½ Lemon, sliced
- Juice from ½ Lemon
- ½ tsp minced Garlic
- 1 tbsp chopped Parsley

Directions

1. Pour the water into the IP and lower the steamer rack.
2. Place the salmon on the rack.
3. Top with garlic and sliced lemons.
4. Close the lid and cook for 4 minutes on HIGH.
5. Do a quick pressure release by switching the pressure valve to "venting".
6. Drizzle the lemon juice over and sprinkle with chopped parsley.
7. Enjoy!

Rich Fish Stew

(Total Time: 20 Min|Serves: 2)

Ingredients

- 1 tbsp Butter
- ¼ Onion, diced
- 1/3 cup frozen Corn
- 2 Potatoes, cubed
- 1 Carrot, sliced
- 1 ½ cups Fish Stock
- 1 Celery Stalk, chopped
- ½ pound Fish Fillets, chopped
- Salt and Pepper, to taste
- 1 Bay Leaf
- ¼ cup Heavy Cream

Directions

1. Melt the butter in the IP on SAUTE.
2. Add the onion and cook for 3 minutes.
3. Add everything else but the heavy cream and give it a good stir.
4. Close the lid and set the IP to MANUAL.
5. Cook on HIGH for about 4-5 minutes.
6. Wait for the pressure to come down naturally.
7. Discard the bay leaf and stir in the cream.
8. Serve and enjoy!

Acorn Squash with Pork Chops

(Total Time: 20Min|Serves: 4)

Ingredients

- 2 tablespoons of clarified butter
- 4 pieces of ½ inch thick bone-in pork loin or rib
- ½ teaspoon of salt
- Pepper, to taste
- 2 medium sized accord squash, peeled and seeded, gently cut into eights
- 3 tablespoons of dried sage
- ½ a teaspoon of dried thyme
- ½ teaspoon of ground cinnamon
- ¾ cup of chicken broth

Directions:

1. Set your pot to Sauté mode and melt 1 tablespoon of butter in it.
2. Season your chops with pepper and salt – add to your pot and cook for 4 minutes.
3. Transfer the chops to a plate and repeat to cook and brown the rest.
4. Then, add in the chops in a single layer and toss in the squash, sprinkle some maple syrup, thyme, sage and cinnamon over it.
5. Pour in the broth then close and lock the lid.
6. Cook for about 10 minutes at HIGH pressure.
7. Quick release the pressure and transfer the chops to a plate.
8. Mound the squash around them nicely and ladle up the sauce over the chops.

Innocent Korean Short Ribs

(Total Time: 55 Min|Serves: 6)

Ingredients

- 5 pounds of bone-in English style short ribs
- 1 tablespoon of kosher salt
- ¼ teaspoon of freshly ground black pepper
- ½ a cup of coconut aminos
- 1 tablespoon of rice vinegar

- 2 teaspoons of Red Boat Fish Sauce
- 1 medium sized Asian Pear
- 6 peeled and roughly chopped garlic cloves
-

- 3 roughly chopped scallions
- 1 hunk of fresh ginger cut up into 2-inch pieces
- Small handful of roughly chopped fresh cilantro

Directions:

1. Pat the ribs well using a kitchen towel.
2. Season them with salt and pepper.
3. Transfer the seasoned ribs to the pot and add coconut aminos, vinegar, fish sauce, pear, scallions, garlic and ginger to a blender.
4. Blitz the mixture well and pour the mixture over the ribs.
5. Stir and lock up the lid and cook on HIGH pressure for about 45 minutes.
6. Release the pressure naturally.
7. Open the lid and check if the meat is fork tender, if not cook for 5-10 minutes more.
8. Transfer the ribs to a serving platter alongside the cooking liquid.
9. Ski the fat using a spoon and spoon the sauce over the ribs.
10. Garnish with a bit of cilantro and enjoy!

Steak with Veggies

(Total Time: 40 Min|Serves: 2)

Ingredients

- ½ pound Round Steak, cubed
- 1 tbsp Flour
- 1 tbsp Butter
- 2 Bell Peppers, chopped
- ½ cup sliced Mushrooms

- 2 Potatoes, cubed
- 1 Carrot, chopped
- ½ tsp Salt
- ¼ tsp Pepper
- 1 ½ cups Beef Broth

Directions

1. Place the steak and flour in a bowl and toss to coat it well.

2. Melt the butter in the Instant Pot.

3. Cook the steak until browned on all sides.

4. Add the vegetables, salt, pepper, and pour the broth over.

5. Lock the lid.

6. Cook on MEAT/STEW for 35 minutes.

7. Do a quick pressure release by switching the pressure valve to "venting".

8. Serve and enjoy!

Cordon Bleu Pasta

(Total Time: 50 Min|Serves: 2)

Ingredients

- 4 ounces Pasta
- ½ pounds Chicken Breasts, cut into strips
- ¼ pounds diced Ham
- 1 cup Chicken Broth
- ¼ cup Breadcrumbs
- 2 ounces Gouda Cheese
- 2 ounces Heavy Cream
- 4 ounces Swiss Cheese
- 1 tbsp Butter

Directions

1. Place the pasta, chicken, ham, and broth, in the Instant Pot.

2. Stir to combine.

3. Cook on HIGH for 25 minutes.

4. Do a quick release by switching the pressure valve to "venting".

5. Add the rest of the ingredients.

6. Stir well and let sit until the cheese is melted.

7. Serve and enjoy!

Herb-Loaded Instant Meatloaf

(Total Time: 30 Min | Serves: 2)

Ingredients

- 1 ½ cups Water
- ¾ pounds ground Beef
- 3 tbsp Breadcrumbs
- 1 Egg
- 1 tsp Parsley
- 1 tsp Thyme

- 1 tsp Oregano
- ½ tsp Rosemary
- ½ tsp Garlic Powder
- ¼ tsp Onion Powder
- ¼ tsp Pepper
- ¼ tsp Salt

Directions

1. Pour the water into the Instant Pot and lower the trivet.
2. Grease a loaf pan with cooking spray.
3. Place all of the ingredients in a large bowl.
4. Mix with your hands to combine.
5. Transfer the mixture to the greased pan.
6. Place the pan on the trivet and close the lid of the IP.
7. Set the Instant Pot to MANUAL.
8. Cook on HIGH for 30 minutes.
9. Do a quick pressure release by switching the pressure valve to "venting".
10. Serve and enjoy!

Sweet Pineapple Glazed Ham

(Total Time: 30 Min | Serves: 2)

Ingredients

- 1-pound Ham
- 2 tbsp Brown Sugar
- ¼ tsp ground Cloves
-

- 2 tbsp Honey
- 2 tbsp crushed Pineapple
- 1 ½ cups Water

Directions

1. Slice a few slits into the ham.
2. Season it with brown sugar and cloves, and then brush the honey over it.
3. Top the ham with the pineapple.
4. Pour the water into the IP and lower the rack.
5. Place the ham on the rack.
6. Close the lid and choose MANUAL.
7. Cook on HIGH for 15 minutes.
8. Let the pressure release naturally.
9. Serve and enjoy!

Gentle Giant's Beef Stroganoff

(Total Time: 25 Min|Serves:4)

Ingredients

- 3 tablespoon of olive oil
- 2 cups of beef strip
- ¼ teaspoon of salt
- ¼ teaspoon of pepper
- 1 tablespoon of almond flour
- 1 chopped up onion
- 2 minced up garlic cloves
- 1 cup of sliced mushroom
- 2 tablespoon of tomato paste
- 3 tablespoon of Worcestershire sauce
- 2 cups of beef broth
- 1 and a ½ cup of zucchini zoodles

Directions:

1. Take a bowl and add in the salt, pepper and flour alongside the beef strips.
2. Coat the beef with the flour and the seasoning.
3. Set your instant pot on LOW heat and LOW pressure and heat the oil.
4. Place your meat in your inner pot and cook for 10 minutes.
5. Add in the rest of your ingredients in your pot.
6. Close up the lid and let it cook for about 18 minutes at medium pressure.
7. Once done, release the pressure naturally.
8. Serve finally alongside a good bunch of zoodles.

The Perfect English Stew

(Total Time: 15 Min | Serves: 6)

Ingredients

- 2 tablespoons of clarified butter
- 1 giant onion peeled up and diced
- 4 large carrots and peeled up and dice
- 4 medium sized potatoes peeled and reduced to half
- 2 celery stalks diced up
- 1 pound of firm flesh white fish fillets reduce to half size
- 2 cups of fish broth
- 1 cup of chilly water
- 1 piece of bay leaf
- Half a teaspoon of dried thyme
- Salt and freshly ground white or black pepper
- Fresh parsley

Directions

1. Set your pot to Sauté mode and add clarified butter, allow it to heat up.
2. Add onion and sauté for 3 minutes.
3. Stir in carrot, potatoes, celery and sauté for 1 minute.
4. Add fish, thyme, bay leaf and pour fish stock.
5. Lock up the lid and cook on HIGH pressure for 4 minutes.
6. Once done, release the pressure and discard the bay leaf.
7. Season with some pepper and salt.
8. Serve by garnishing with parsley.

Smothered Barbecue Ribs with Cinnamon

(Total Time: 85 Min | Serves: 2)

Ingredients

- ½ Onion, diced
- 1 ½ pounds Pork Ribs
- 1 tbsp ground Cloves
- ½ tbsp Brown Sugar
- ½ cup Barbecue Sauce
- ¼ cup Apple Jelly
- 1 tsp Worcestershire Sauce
- ¼ cup Water

- ½ tsp Cinnamon

Directions

1. Whisk all of the ingredients (except the ribs) in the Instant Pot.
2. Add the ribs inside and close the lid.
3. Cook on POULTRY for 60 minutes.
4. Let the pressure come down naturally.
5. Serve as desired and enjoy!

Taco Pie

(Total Time: 20 Min|Serves: 2)

Ingredients

- 3 Corn tortillas
- 6 ounces Mexican Cheese Blend
- ½ packed Taco Seasoning
- ½ pound Ground Beef
- ½ cup canned Beans
- 1 ½ cups Water

Directions

1. Pour the water in the IP and lower the trivet.
2. Grease a small baking dish with cooking spray.
3. In a bowl, combine the beef, beans, 2/3 of the cheese, and seasonings.
4. Lay out one tortilla in the greased dish and top with half of the beef mixture.
5. Add another tortilla on top and spread the remaining mixture over.
6. Top with the third tortilla and sprinkle with the remaining cheese.
7. Place the dish on the trivet and close the lid.
8. Cook on HIGH for 12 minutes.
9. Do a quick pressure release by switching the pressure valve to "venting".
10. Serve and enjoy!

Tuna Noodles with Peas and Cheese

(Total Time: 20 Min|Serves: 2)

Ingredients

- 1 ½ cups Water
- 8 ounces Egg Noodles
- ½ cup Frozen Peas
- 1 can Tuna, drained
- 14 ounces canned Mushroom Soup
- 2 ounces grated Cheddar Cheese
- 2 tbsp Breadcrumbs

Directions

1. Combine the noodles and water in your IP.
2. Stir in the peas, tuna, and soup.
3. Close the lid and choose POULTRY.
4. Cook for 5 minutes.
5. Do a quick pressure release by switching the pressure valve to "venting"..
6. Drain the pasta and transfer to a greased baking dish.
7. Sprinkle with the cheese and breadcrumbs.
8. Place the dish in the IP and close the lid.
9. Cook on HIGH for 1 minute.
10. Do a quick pressure release again.
11. Serve and enjoy!

Chili Lime Chicken with Rice

(Total Time: 35 Min|Serves: 2)

Ingredients

- ¼ cup Tomato Sauce
- 3 tbsp Olive Oil
- ¼ cup Salsa
- ¼ cup Lime Juice
- 2 Frozen Chicken Breast
- ¼ cup Mexican Cheese Blend
- ½ cup Rice
- 2/3 cup Water

Directions

1. Combine tomato sauce, oil, salsa, and lime juice.

2. Add the chicken and cheese then close the lid.
3. Cook on HIGH for 13 minutes.
4. Do a natural pressure release.
5. Transfer the chicken to a plate.
6. Stir in the rice and water.
7. Close the lid and cook for 12 minutes on HIGH.
8. Do a quick pressure release by switching the pressure valve to "venting".
9. Serve the chicken with rice. Enjoy!

Spaghetti Squash "Cooked"

(Total Time: 17 Min|Serves: 2)

Ingredients

- 1 medium sized spaghetti squash
- 1 cup of water

Directions

1. Cut the spaghetti squash half and then crosswise using a paring knife.
2. Take a large spoon and scoop out the seeds from the center.
3. Add your steamer to the pot with 1 cup water.
4. Add the halves to the steamer insert (make sure to keep the cut side up).
5. Lock up the lid and cook for about 7 minutes at HIGH pressure.
6. Once done, release the pressure naturally.
7. Remove the lid and tip the squashes over (pour out the liquid as well) to your serving bowl.
8. Shred the squash with fork and voila!

Extremely Juicy Apple BBQ Ribs

(Total Time: 45 Min|Serves: 8)

Ingredients

- 4 cups of apple juice
- ½ a cup of apple cider vinegar
- 3 pounds of Racks of ribs, fat completely trimmed up
- 1 tablespoon of salt
- ½ a tablespoon of black pepper
- ½ a tablespoon of garlic powder
- Southern Apple Cider BBQ Sauce or the one that you prefer the most!

Directions:

1. Pour apple juice and cider vinegar into your Pot.
2. Set it to Sauté mode and let it heat up.
3. Season both sides of your ribs with salt, garlic powder, and pepper.
4. Rub well with your hand.
5. Cut up the rib into 2 portions and add them to your pot once the apple mixture starts to steam up.
6. Lock up the lid and cook for 30 minutes.
7. Once cooking is complete, allow the pressure to release naturally over 10 minutes.
8. Pre-heat your oven to 400-degrees Fahrenheit.
9. Take a baking pan and carefully cover it using an aluminum foil.
10. Transfer the cooker ribs on top of your foil.
11. Spread 1 tablespoon of BBQ sauce on either side of your ribs.
12. Cook for about 5 minutes in your oven and serve!

Astonishing Vegetable Chicken Breast

(Total Time: 50 Min|Serves: 4)

Ingredients

- 2 whole chicken breasts
- 1 teaspoon of salt
- 1 teaspoon of black pepper
- Olive oil, as needed

- ½ a cup of chicken broth
- 2 cups of carrots
- 8 medium sized new potatoes
- 1 cup of pearl onion
- 1 spring rosemary
- 1 pieces of spring thyme
- 2 pieces of minced cloves of garlic

Directions:

1. Season the chicken breast with pepper and salt.
2. Spread olive oil on bottom of the pot.
3. Carefully pour the chicken broth to the pot.
4. Stir well and add the chicken breast.
5. Add layers of thyme, garlic, onion and rosemary.
6. Top up with potatoes and carrots and season with salt and pepper.
7. Lock up the lid and cook on MEAT setting for 40 minutes.
8. Allow the cooker to release the pressure naturally. Enjoy!

Vegetarian Burger Patties

(Total Time: 30 Min|Serves: 2)

Ingredients

- 1 tbsp Olive Oil
- 1 small onion, diced
- 1 cup Sweet Potato cubes
- 1 Carrot, grated
- 2/3 cup Veggie Broth
- ½ Zucchini, grated
- 1 ½ cups Cauliflower Florets
- 1 cup Broccoli Florets
- ¼ tsp Turmeric
- ¼ tsp Pepper
- ¼ tsp Salt

Directions

1. Heat the oil in the IP on SAUTE.
2. Add onion and cook for 2 minutes.
3. Add the sweet potatoes and carrots and cook for one more minute.
4. Pour the broth over then add the zucchini, cauliflower, and broccoli.
5. Close the lid and cook on POULTRY for 10 minutes.
6. Do a quick pressure release and add the remaining veggies.

7. Cook for another 3 minutes on HIGH.
8. Mash everything with a potato masher and season with salt, turmeric, and pepper.
9. Make 2 patties from the mixture.
10. Discard the cooking liquid, wipe the pot clean, and coat with cooking spray.
11. Add patties and cook until golden on all sides.
12. Serve and enjoy!

Tilapia and Tomatoes

(Total Time: 15 Min|Serves: 2)

Ingredients

- 1 cup chopped Tomatoes
- Salt and Pepper, to taste
- 2 Tilapia Fillets
- 1 tbsp Olive Oil
- ¼ tsp Garlic Powder
- ¼ tsp Basil
- 1 cup Water

Directions

1. In a greased baking dish, place the tomatoes and mash with a fork.
2. Season with some salt and pepper.
3. Place the tilapia on top.
4. Season again and sprinkle with garlic powder and basil.
5. Drizzle with the olive oil.
6. Pour the water into the Instant Pot.
7. Lower the trivet and place the dish on top of it.
8. Close the li and cook on HIGH for 5 minutes.
9. Release the pressure after 5 minutes.
10. Serve and enjoy!

The Supreme Pork Shoulder

(Total Time: 65 Min|Serves: 6)

Ingredients

- ¼ cup of orange juice
- ½ a teaspoon of ground cumin
- ¼ cup of lime juice
- 5 minced garlic cloves
- 1 teaspoon of salt
- 3 pound of boneless pork shoulder cut up into 2-inch cubes
- Chopped up fresh cilantro

Directions:

1. Add orange juice, cumin, lime juice, garlic and salt to your pot.
2. Add pork to the pot and toss well.
3. Lock up the lid and cook on HIGH pressure for 45 minutes.
4. Allow the pressure to release naturally over 10 minutes.
5. Pre-heat your broiler.
6. Take the pork out using tong and place it on a baking sheet.
7. Set the pot to Sauté mode and allow the liquid to reduce for about 10-15 minutes.
8. Pour liquid into a heatproof dish.
9. Broil your pork for about 3-5 minutes per side until crispy and serve the broiled pork with the sauce. Enjoy!

Mesmerizing Braised Kale and Carrots

(Total Time: 10 Min|Serves: 8)

Ingredients

- 1 tablespoon of ghee
- 3 medium sized carrots cut up into ½ inch slices
- 1 medium sized thinly sliced onion
- 5 cloves of garlic, peeled up and roughly chopped
- 10 ounces of roughly chopped kale
- ½ a cup of chicken broth
- Kosher salt as needed
- Freshly ground pepper
- Aged balsamic vinegar
- ¼ teaspoon of red pepper flakes

Directions

1. Set your pot to Sauté mode and add ghee.
2. Add chopped up carrots and onion and sauté until tender.
3. Add garlic and stir for 30 seconds.
4. Pile the kale on top and pour chicken broth.
5. Sprinkle a bit of salt and pepper.
6. Set it to HIGH pressure and cook for 5 minutes.
7. Release the pressure naturally and mix well.
8. Season with a bit of salt and pepper.
9. Splash balsamic vinegar and sprinkle red pepper flakes and enjoy!

Chard and Mushroom Risotto

(Total Time: 15 Min|Serves: 2)

Ingredients

- 1 tbsp Olive Oil
- ¼ Onion, chopped
- 1 tsp minced Garlic
- ½ cup Arborio Rice
- ¼ cup White Wine
- 4 ounces sliced Mushrooms
- ½ tsp Thyme
- 1 ½ cups Vegetable Broth
- 2 tbsp Lemon Juice
- ¾ tbsp Nutritional Yeast
- 1 tbsp Butter
- 1 cup chopped Chard

Directions

1. Heat the oil in your Instant Pot on SAUTE.
2. Add onions and cook until soft.
3. Add garlic and cook for 30 seconds more.
4. Add the rice, wine, mushrooms, thyme, and lemon juice, and stir to combine.
5. Pour the broth over and close the lid.
6. Cook on HIGH for 6 minutes.
7. Do a quick pressure release.
8. Stir in the yeast, butter, and chard.
9. Serve and enjoy!

Ever So Brilliant Mango Chicken

(Total Time: 20 Min|Serves: 6)

Ingredients

- 1 cup water
- 4 pieces of chicken breast
- Salt as needed

- 14 ounce of mango chunky salsa
- 1 piece of fresh mango
- Jamaican hot sauce

Directions:

1. Add 1 cup of water to your pot and season the chicken breast with salt.
2. Add the breast on a steamer rack and pour half of the salsa on top of your chicken.
3. Place the steamer rack (with the chicken) on top of your cooker and lock up the lid.
4. Cook for 15 minutes at HIGH pressure and allow the pressure to release naturally over 10 minutes.
5. Remove the chicken, drain it out of the water.
6. Add the chicken back to your pot alongside any salsa.
7. Add hot sauce and shred the chicken.
8. Dice up mango and add them to the pot.
9. Mix well and serve!

Beef Bourguignon

(Total Time: 60 Min|Serves: 2)

Ingredients

- 1 tbsp Olive Oil
- ¼ Red Onion, sliced
- ½ pound Beef chunks
- ¼ pound Bacon Tips
- ½ cup Red Wine

- ½ tbsp Maple Syrup
- ½ cup Beef Broth
- 1 Carrot, sliced
- 1 Sweet Potato, cubed
- Salt and Pepper, to taste

Directions

1. Heat the oil in the IP on SAUTE.
2. Add onion and cook for 2 minutes.
3. Add the beef and cook until browned.
4. Stir in the bacon tips and cook for another 2 minutes.
5. Add the remaining ingredients and stir everything well.
6. Close the lid and cook for 30 minutes n HIGH.
7. Let the pressure drop naturally, for about 10 minutes.
8. Serve and enjoy!

Asian Salmon and Veggies

(Total Time: 15 Min|Serves: 4)

Ingredients:

For Fish

- 2 medium sized salmon fillets
- 1 clove of finely diced garlic
- ¼ long red chili finely diced
- Sea salt as needed

- Pepper as needed
- 1 teaspoon of honey
- 2 tablespoon of tamari sauce

For Veggies

- 7 ounce of mixed green vegetables
- 1 large sized sliced carrot
- 1 diced clove of garlic
- Juice of ½ a lime

- 1 tablespoon of tamari sauce
- 1 tablespoon of olive oil
- ½ a teaspoon of sesame oil

Preparation:

1. Add 1 cup of water to your pot and place the steamer rack inside.
2. Add fillets to a heat proof bowl and sprinkle with garlic, chili, salt, and pepper.
3. Take a small bowl and add honey and tamari sauce and pour over the fillets.
4. Set the salmon bowl in your steamer rack and lock up the lid.
5. Allow it cook for about 3 minutes under HIGH pressure.
6. Cut the vegetables and place them in a steam basket, season with some salt.
7. Release the pressure quickly by switching the pressure valve to "venting".

8. Transfer the steam basket with the veggies on top of your salmon bowl.

9. Drizzle the veggies with lime juice, olive oil, tamari sauce, sesame oil and season with a bit of salt and pepper.

10. Lock up the lid and set HIGH pressure, wait for a minute and quick release.

11. Remove the steamer basket with veggies and keep it on the side.

12. Remove the bowl the salmon and transfer it to your plate.

13. Pour any leftover juice on top and serve with the veggies!

Pastrami from the Instant Pot

(Total Time: 55 Min|Serves: 2)

Ingredients

- 1 ½ cups Water
- ¾ pounds Corned Beef
- 2 tbsp Olive Oil
- ¾ tsp Paprika
- ¼ tsp Cloves
- 1 tsp Onion Powder
- 1 tsp Garlic Powder
- 1 tsp Brown Sugar
- 1 tsp Pepper
- 1 tsp Salt

Directions

1. Pour the water into the pot and lower the trivet.
2. Add the beef to the Instant Pot and close the lid.
3. Cook on HIGH for 45 minutes.
4. Meanwhile, combine the oil and spices.
5. Brush the mixture over the meat.
6. When the meat is done, quick release pressure by switching the pressure valve to "venting".
7. Discard the water from the IP and wipe it clean.
8. Set it to SAUTE.
9. Add beef and sear for one minute per side.
10. Serve and enjoy!

Instant Lasagna

(Total Time: 40 Min|Serves: 2)

Ingredients

- ¼ Onion, diced
- ½ pound ground Beef
- 12 ounces Tomato Sauce
- 1 tsp Italian Seasoning
- 3 ounces shredded Mozzarella Cheese

- ¾ pound Ricotta Cheese
- 1 Egg
- 2 tbsp grated Parmesan Cheese
- 8 ounces Lasagna Noodles

Directions

1. Coat the IP with cooking spray.
2. Add onions and cook for 2 minutes.
3. Add beef and cook until browned.
4. Stir in the tomato sauce, half of the Italian seasoning - transfer to a bowl.
5. In another bowl, combine the ricotta, remaining seasoning, egg, and parmesan.
6. Add about ¼ inch of water in the IP.
7. Add some of the beef sauce and arrange 1/3 of the noodles.
8. Spread 1/3 of the ricotta mixture over the noodles.
9. Add some of the beef mixture on top.
10. Repeat the layers until you use all of the ingredients.
11. Top with mozzarella cheese.
12. Close the lid and cook the lasagna on HIGH for 7 minutes.
13. Quick release the pressure by switching the pressure valve to "venting".
14. Serve and enjoy!

A Salsa Chicken Full Of Magic

(Total Time: 25 Min|Serves: 8)

Ingredients

- 1 pound of chicken breast
- 1 and a ½ cup of salsa
- ½ a teaspoon of sea salt
- ¼ teaspoon of black pepper
- ½ a teaspoon of onion powder
- ½ a teaspoon of garlic powder
- Cumin powder as needed
- Freshly diced jalapeno (seeded)
- Avocado slices for serving
- Cilantro for garnish

Directions:

1. Add the ingredients to your pot and season it well.
2. Lock up the lid and cook on HIGH pressure for 15 minutes.
3. Do a quick release by switching the pressure valve to "venting".
4. Shred the chicken using fork and serve with avocado slices and a bit of cilantro.

Ketchup Glazed Pork Meatloaf

(Total Time: 50 Min|Serves: 2)

Ingredients

- 1/3 pound Ground Sausage
- 1/3 pound Ground Pork
- 1/2 cup cooked Rice
- ¼ cup Milk
- 1 Egg, beaten
- 1/4 tsp Cayenne Pepper
-
- ½ tsp minced Garlic
- ½ Onion, diced
- ¼ tsp Marjoram
- 1 cup Ketchup
- 2 tbsp Brown Sugar

Directions

1. Place all of the ingredients, except the ketchup and sugar, in a large bowl.
2. Mix well with your hands to incorporate the ingredients.

3. Shape the meat mixture into a log shape, to make a classic meatloaf.
4. Place the meatloaf inside the IP.
5. Combine the sugar and ketchup in a bowl and pour the mixture over the meatloaf.
6. Close the lid and choose MEAT/STEW.
7. Cook for 40 minutes.
8. Release the pressure quickly by switching the pressure valve to "venting".
9. Serve and enjoy!

Delicious Pot of Indian Saag
(Total Time: 20 Min|Serves: 4)

Ingredients

- 2 tablespoons of ghee
- 4 cloves of minced garlic cloves
- 2 medium sized diced onion
- 1 pound of rinsed spinach
- 1 pound of rinsed mustard leaves
- 2-inch knob ginger of minced
- 2 teaspoons of salt

- 1 teaspoon of coriander
- 1 teaspoon of cumin
- 1 teaspoon of Garam masala
- ½ a teaspoon of turmeric
- ½ a teaspoon of cayenne
- ½ a teaspoon of black pepper
- Just a pinch of kasoori methi

Directions

1. Set your pot to Sauté mode and allow the ghee to melt.
2. Once ghee has melted, add garlic, onion, spinach, and spices and give it a nice stir and fry for 2-3 minutes.
3. Lock up the lid and cook for 15 minutes on the POULTRY setting.
4. Once the cooking is done, allow the pressure to release naturally over 10 minutes.
5. Add the pot contents to a blender and blend well.
6. Alternatively, you may use an immersion blender to blend them well until you have reached your desire consistency.
7. Serve with a topping of ghee and enjoy!

Ground Beef, Sauerkraut & Leek

(Total Time: 40 Min|Serves: 2)

Ingredients

- 1 tbsp Butter
- 1/3 cup sliced Leeks
- 2/3 pound Ground Beef
- 5 ounces canned Tomato Sauce
- ½ tsp Mustard Powder
- 1 cup Sauerkraut
- Salt and Pepper, to taste

Directions

1. Set your Instant Pot to SAUTE and melt the butter in it.
2. Add the leeks and sauté for a couple of minutes.
3. Add the ground beef and cook for 4 minutes, or until it becomes brown.
4. Stir in the remaining ingredients and season with some salt and pepper.
5. Close the lid and cook on MANUAL for 15 minutes.
6. Do a quick pressure release by switching the pressure valve to "venting".
7. Serve and enjoy!

Enchilada Casserole

(Total Time: 40 Min|Serves: 2)

Ingredients

- 1 Shallot, diced
- 2/3 pounds Ground Beef
- 1 jalapeno pepper, seeded and minced
- ¼ tsp Cumin
- ½ tsp Chili Powder
- 4 ounces Enchilada Sauce
- 5 ounces canned Mushroom Soup
- 4 ounces canned Celery Soup
- 5 ounces shredded Cheddar Cheese
- 1 cup canned black beans
- 4 ounces Tortilla Chips

Directions

1. Grease the IP with cooking spray and sauté the shallots until soft.
2. Add beef and cook until the meat turns brown.

3. Stir in the jalapeno, cumin, and chili powder, and cook for another minute or two.
4. Add the soups and sauce and stir to combine.
5. Close the lid and cook on HIGH for 15 minutes.
6. Do a quick pressure release.
7. Top with the chips and cheese, close the lid again, and cook for another 5 minutes on HIGH.
8. Release the pressure quickly by switching the pressure valve to "venting".
9. Serve and enjoy!

Sloppy Joes

(Total Time: 40 Min|Serves: 2)

Ingredients

- ½ pounds Ground Beef
- ¼ tsp Chili Powder
- ½ Tomato, diced
- ¼ cup Barley
- 1 tbsp Ketchup
- 1 tbsp Worcestershire Sauce
- 2 tbsp diced Shallots
- 1/4 tsp Cayenne Pepper
- 2/3 cup Water
- 1 tsp Canola Oil
- 1 tsp Brown Sugar
- 2 Kaiser Rolls

Directions

1. Place all of the ingredients, except the rolls, inside your Instant Pot.
2. Stir to combine and close the lid.
3. Cook on MEAT/STEW for 30 minutes.
4. Do a quick pressure release by switching the pressure valve to "venting".
5. Divide the mixture between the rolls.
6. Serve and enjoy!

Vegetable Chowder

(Total Time: 35 Min|Serves: 2)

Ingredients

- 1 tbsp Coconut Oil
- 1/2 Onion, diced
- 1 cup Corn
- 2 Potatoes, cubed
- 1 Large Carrot, sliced
- ¼ tsp Cumin
- ¼ tsp Paprika

- ¼ tsp Garlic Salt
- ¼ tsp Pepper
- ½ tbsp Potato Starch
- 2/3 cup Coconut Milk
- 1 ½ cups Veggie Broth
- 1 cup Green Beans

Directions

1. Melt the coconut oil in your IP on SAUTE.
2. Add the onion and corn and cook until the onions become soft.
3. Stir in the potatoes, carrots, and spices. Cook for another minute.
4. Add the remaining ingredients and stir to combine.
5. Close the lid and choose MANUAL.
6. Cook on HIGH for 15 minutes.
7. Let the pressure drop on its own.
8. Serve and enjoy!

Creamy Haddock with Cheese

(Total Time: 35 Min|Serves: 2)

Ingredients

- 2 Haddock Fillets
- ¼ tsp Garlic Powder
- Salt and Pepper, to taste
- 1 tbsp Butter
- ½ cup Heavy Cream
- 4 ounces shredded Cheddar Cheese

Directions

1. Season the haddock with garlic powder, salt, and pepper.
2. Set your IP to SAUTE and melt the butter in it.
3. Add the haddock and cook it for about 2 minutes on each side.
4. Pour the heavy cream over and sprinkle with cheese.
5. Close the lid and set the IP to MANUAL.
6. Cook on HIGH for 3 minutes.
7. Do a quick pressure release by switching the pressure valve to "venting".
8. Serve and enjoy!

The Divine Thai Brisket Curry

(Total Time: 45 Min|Serves: 9)

Ingredients

- 3 pounds of grass fed beef brisket
- 2 teaspoons of kosher salt
- 1 tablespoon of Thai curry paste
- 1 and a ½ cup of full fat coconut milk (additional ½ a cup)
- 2 tablespoons of apple juice (won't cause trouble in such small amount)
- 1 tablespoon of Red Boat Fish Sauce
- 2 tablespoons of coconut aminos
- 2 medium sweet potatoes
- 2 small peeled and coarsely chopped onion
- 2 large peeled carrots cut up into 2-inch pieces
- Just a handful of mixed herbs (cilantro and scallions)

Directions:

1. Take a large bowl and add cubed beef and season it well with salt.
2. Set your pot to Sauté mode and heat up the coconut oil.
3. Add curry paste and stir it well.
4. Pour coconut milk, apple juice, fish sauce, coconut aminos and stir well.

5. Add onion, beef cubes, potatoes and carrots and stir well.
6. Lock up the lid and cook on MEAT setting for 35 minutes.
7. Release the pressure naturally and transfer the meat to a serving platter.
8. Pour vegetables and sauce into the blender with ½ cup of additional coconut milk.
9. Puree the sauce until smooth.
10. Pour the sauce over your beef and serve!

Pepperoni Pizza Pasta

(Total Time: 15 Min|Serves: 2)

Ingredients

- 1 tbsp Butter
- 1 Garlic Clove, minced
- 1/3 pounds sliced Sausages
- 8 Pepperoni Slices
- 3 ounces shredded Mozzarella Cheese
- 1/3 pounds Pasta
- 5 ounces Pizza Sauce
- 3 ounces Pasta Sauce
- ½ tsp Italian Seasoning

Directions

1. Melt the butter in the IP on SAUTE.
2. Add garlic and cook for 30 seconds.
3. Add sausage and cook until it becomes browned.
4. Stir in half of the pepperoni, half of the cheese, the pasta, and the sauces.
5. Close and lock the lid and set it to MANUAL.
6. Cook on HIGH for 5 minutes.
7. Release the pressure quickly by switching the pressure valve to "venting".
8. Stir in the remaining pepperoni.
9. Top with the remaining mozzarella.
10. Serve and enjoy!

Chili with Turkey

(Total Time: 50 Min|Serves: 2)

Ingredients

- 1 tbsp Olive Oil
- 1 Bell Pepper, chopped
- ½ Onion, chopped
- 1 tsp minced Garlic
- ½ pound Ground Turkey
- ¼ tsp Oregano
- ½ can Beans, drained
- ½ can chopped Tomatoes with the juice
- 2 tbsp Hot Sauce
- ½ cup Chicken Broth
- ½ cup grated Cheddar Cheese

Directions

1. Set the IP to SAUTE and heat the oil in it.
2. Add the peppers and onion and cook for 5 minutes, or until soft.
3. Add garlic and cook for another minute.
4. Add the turkey and oregano and cook until the turkey turns brown.
5. Stir in everything else, except for the cheese.
6. Close the lid and choose BEANS/CHILI.
7. Choose the default cooking time.
8. Do a natural pressure release.
9. Top with the cheese. Enjoy!

A Touch of Summer Garden Variety Salad

(Total Time: 25 Min|Serves: 5)

Ingredients

- 1 pound of raw peanuts
- 2 cups water
- 1 bay leaf
- 2 medium sized chopped up tomatoes
- ½ a cup of diced up green pepper
- ½ a cup of diced up sweet onion
- ¼ cup of finely diced hot pepper
- ¼ cup of diced up celery
- 2 tablespoon of olive oil
- ¾ teaspoon of salt

- ¼ teaspoon of freshly ground black pepper
-

Directions:

1. Blanch your peanuts in boiling salt water for 1 minute and drain well.
2. The skin will come off, discard it.
3. In your instant pot, add in 2 cups of water and bay leaf and toss in the peanuts.
4. Let it cook for 20 minutes under high pressure.
5. Release the pressure and drain out the water.
6. Take a large bowl and combine the peanuts with the diced vegetables.
7. Whisk in finely some oil, lemon juice, pepper and salt in a bowl.
8. Pour over the salad mixture and keep tossing it to combine nicely.

Auspicious Mexican Meatloaf

(Total Time: 30 Min|Serves: 4)

Ingredients

- 2 pound of ground organic beef
- 1 cup of roasted salsa
- 1 teaspoon of cumin
- 1 teaspoon of chili powder
- 1 teaspoon of garlic
- 1 teaspoon of paprika
- 1 teaspoon of onion powder
- 1 teaspoon of sea salt
- 1 teaspoon of ground black pepper
- 1 diced onion
- 1 pastured egg
- ¼ cup of tapioca start
- 1 tablespoon of ghee

Directions:

1. Take a bowl and add the listed ingredients.
2. Mix well and transfer the mixture to a meatloaf pan.
3. Set your pot to Sauté mode and add a teaspoon of ghee, allow it to melt.
4. Add the meatloaf to your pot and lock the lid.
5. Cook for about 35 minutes on MEAT/STEW settings.
6. Release the pressure naturally.

7. Serve with a sprinkle of cilantro. Enjoy!

Chicken with Tomatoes and Sour Cream

(Total Time: 40 Min|Serves: 2)

Ingredients

- 1 cup Chicken Broth
- 2 Chicken Breasts, boneless and skinless
- ½ cup Sour Cream
- 8 ounces canned Tomatoes, undrained
- Pinch of Garlic Powder
- ¼ tsp Salt
- Pinch of Pepper

Directions

1. Pour the broth into the Instant Pot and place the chicken in it.
2. Close the lid and cook on HIGH for about 20 minutes.
3. Do a quick pressure release and transfer the chicken to a plate.
4. Shred with two forks.
5. Get rid of the IP liquid and set it to SAUTE.
6. Add sour cream, tomatoes, salt, pepper, garlic powder, and shredded chicken.
7. Stir to combine.
8. Cook on SAUTE for 5 minutes.
9. Serve and enjoy!

The Ultimate Smoked Brisket

(Total Time: 55 Min|Serves: 4)

Ingredients

- 1 and a half pound of beef brisket
- 2 teaspoons of salt
- 1 teaspoon of black pepper
- 1 teaspoon of onion powder
- ½ teaspoon of smoked paprika
- 1 teaspoon of mustard powder
- 2 tablespoons of date paste
- 1 tablespoon olive oil

- 2 cup of chicken stock
- 1 tablespoon of liquid smoke
- 3 fresh sprigs of thyme

Directions:

1. Chill your brisket for 30 minutes prior to cooking.
2. Take a bowl and add the salt, pepper, onion powder, smoked paprika, mustard powder and date paste.
3. Mix well to create the spice blend.
4. Take the mixture and coat the brisket on all sides.
5. Set your pot to Sauté mode and add olive oil.
6. Once the oil is hot, add the brisket and brown it all over.
7. Add broth, liquid smoke, and thyme.
8. Once perfectly browned, lock up the lid and cook under HIGH pressure for 50 minutes.
9. Release the pressure naturally.
10. For a thicker sauce, simply remove the brisket and set your pot to Sauté mode.
11. After 10 minutes, the sauce will be thick. Enjoy!

Vegetarian Chili

(Total Time: 35 Min|Serves: 2)

Ingredients

- 1 tbsp Olive Oil
- 1 Bell Pepper, chopped
- ½ Onion, chopped
- ½ tsp minced Garlic
- ½ cup Red Lentils
- 2 ¼ cups Veggie Stock
- 14 ounces canned Tomatoes, diced
- ½ cup French Lentils
- ¼ tsp Salt
- 1 tsp Chili Powder
- ½ tsp Cumin

Directions

1. Set the IP to SAUTE and heat the oil in it.
2. Add peppers and onions and cook for a couple of minutes.

3. Add the garlic and sauté for 30 – 60 seconds.
4. Stir in all of the remaining ingredients.
5. Close and lock the lid.
6. Cook on MANUAL, on HIGH, for 15 minutes.
7. Let the pressure come down naturally.
8. Serve and enjoy!

Garlic and Chicken Patties

(Total Time: 20 Min|Serves: 4)

Ingredients

- 1 pound of ground chicken meat
- 1 cup of almond flour
- 3 pieces of beaten egg
- 2 tablespoon of garlic powder
- 1 tablespoon of black pepper

Directions:

1. Take a bowl and add the listed ingredients to the bowl, mixing well.
2. Add a cup of water to your pot.
3. Take an oven safe dish and line it up with parchment paper.
4. Place the mix in the dish.
5. Take an aluminum foil and cover it up.
6. Transfer it to your pot and lock up the lid.
7. Cook for about 10 minutes at HIGH pressure.
8. Release the pressure naturally, take the meat out and form patties. Enjoy!

The Great Potato Casserole of Beef

(Total Time: 25 Min|Serves: 3)

Ingredients

- 2 tablespoons of butter
- 1 chopped up yellow onion
- 1 pound of ground beef
- 2 cups of cubed up potatoes
- 5 pieces of broccoli florets
- 2 cups of beef broth
- 2 cups of tomato sauce
- 1 cup of Whole30 Mayonnaise

Directions:

1. Set your instant pot to Sauté mode and toss in the onion with the butter.
2. Toss in the beef and set it to HIGH pressure and let it cook for 5 minutes.
3. Release the pressure naturally and stir it well.
4. Toss in the potatoes, broccoli alongside the beef broth.
5. Set the instant pot to HIGH heat and pressure to low and cook it for 5 minutes.
6. Once done, release the pressure naturally and stir in the tomato sauce.
7. Finally top it up wish some mayonnaise. Serve hot.

Dearest Curried Potato Chicken

(Total Time: 35 Min|Serves: 4)

Ingredients

For Marinade

- 4 pound of chicken legs
- 1 teaspoon of garlic powder
- 1 teaspoon of onion powder
- 1 tablespoon of spicy yellow curry powder
- 2 tablespoon of olive oil
- 1 teaspoon of kosher salt

For Curry

- 2 cups of coconut milk
- 1 tablespoon of spicy yellow curry powder
- 1 cup of water
- 4 cups of peeled potatoes cut up into 1.5-inch chunks
- ¼ cups of chopped dates
- ¼ cup of chopped cilantro
- ¼ cup of sliced fresh jalapenos

Directions:

1. Take a large bowl and add the marinade ingredients and mix well.
2. Add the chicken and toss to coat it then chill overnight.
3. Set your pot to Sauté mode and add the chicken and brown it.
4. Add 2 cups of coconut milk, 1 tablespoon of yellow curry powder, ¼ cup of dates, 4 cups of potatoes to your pot.
5. Lock up the cooker and allow it to cook for 25 minutes under HIGH pressure.
6. Release the pressure naturally.
7. Remove the chicken and potatoes and transfer them to your serving plate.
8. Set your pot to Sauté mode and simmer the liquid for 5 minutes to thicken it.
9. Pour the sauce over your chicken and garnish with a bit of cilantro. Enjoy!

Yet Another Crispy Potato recipe
(Total Time: 12 Min|Serves: 4)

Ingredients

- 1 pound of fingerling potatoes (peeled and cut into 1 ½ inch cubes)
- 2 tablespoons of ghee
- Salt as needed
- Freshly ground black pepper
- ¼ cup of minced Italian parsley
- ½ a medium lemon

Directions

1. Add ½ a cup of water to the pot then add the potatoes.
2. Lock up the lid and allow them to cook for about 5 minutes under HIGH pressure.
3. Allow the pressure to release naturally.
4. Take a large skillet and place it over medium high heat.
5. Add ghee and allow it to melt.
6. Once done, add the potatoes to the pan.
7. Season with some pepper and salt and leave them for 1 minute.

8. Flip them and cook for 1 minute more.
9. Squeeze a bit of lemon juice and add fresh Italian parsley. Stir and serve!

Ravishing Pumpkin Soup

(Total Time:20Min|Serves: 4)

Ingredients

- 2 tablespoons of clarified butter
- 1 piece of chopped onion
- 3 tablespoons of almond flour
- 2 tablespoon of curry powder
- 4 cups of low sodium vegetable broth
- 1 cup of water
- 4 cups of fresh pumpkin puree
- 2 tablespoon of coconut aminos
- 1 teaspoon of lemon juice
- Just a pinch cayenne pepper
- Salt as needed
- Pepper as needed
- 1 and a ½ cups of fat free half and half

Directions:

1. Set your pot to Sauté mode.
2. Add clarified butter and allow the butter to heat up.
3. Add onion and cook them for a few minutes until brown.
4. Add flour and curry powder and stir until smooth.
5. Once it begins to bubble, add water and broth.
6. Stir in pumpkin, coconut aminos, pepper and salt.
7. Cook for 3 minutes at HIGH pressure.
8. Quick release the pressure and remove the lid.
9. Set your cooker to Sauté mode again and stir in fat-free half and half.
10. Blend the soup using an immersion blender and bring the soup to a boil.
11. Turn the heat off and stir in a bit of lemon juice. Enjoy!

Tender Soft Pumpkin Pies

(Total Time: 15 Min|Serves: 4)

Ingredients

- 2 pounds of peeled and diced butter nut squash
- 4 cups milk
- 2 large eggs
- 1 teaspoon of powdered cinnamon
- ½ a teaspoon of powdered ginger
- ¼ teaspoon of powdered cloves
- 1 tablespoon of organic corn starch
- 2 pinches of salt

For garnish

- Chopped up pecans

Directions:

1. Add 1 cup of water into the instant pot.
2. Toss in the squash cubes into the steamer basket and lower the pressure.
3. Close the lid and let it cook for about 3-4 minutes at high pressure.
4. While it is being cooked, take a medium mixing bowl and pour in 4 cups of milk.
5. Toss in the cinnamon, eggs, ginger, corn starch and salt and puree using an immersion blender.
6. Once the squash is cooked, take a fine mesh strainer and strain the cooled squash, reserving the juice.
7. Gently take the pulp into 2 cups and freeze them.
8. Take the pulp and pour them into the egg mixture.
9. In your instant pot, add about 1 cup of water.
10. Pour in the previously made mixture into a nice heat proof ramekin and lower it into the cooker.
11. Make sure to put the second layer on top of the first layer making sure to balance out the edges of the ramekin below.
12. Close the lid of the cooker and let it cook for 10 minutes on HIGH pressure.
13. Let the pressure release naturally.
14. Take out the ramekins and let them stand for 5 minutes before serving.

Chapter 3: Dinner Recipes

Delicious Prosciutto Wrapped Cane
(Total Time: 8Min|Serves: 4)

Ingredients

- 1 pound of thick asparagus
- 80 ounce of thinly sliced prosciutto

Directions

1. Add 2 cups of water to your pot
2. Place a steamer rack on top of your pot
3. Wrap the asparagus into prosciutto spears
4. Place the wrapped asparagus in the steamer basket
5. Lock up the lid and cook on HIGH pressure for 2-3 minutes
6. Allow the pressure to release naturally
7. Take out the asparagus spears and serve.

Refreshing Turkey Meal
(Total Time: 75 Min|Serves: 6)

Ingredients

- 1 piece of 4-5 pound bone-in skin on turkey breast
- Salt
- Black pepper
- 2 tablespoon butter/ghee
- 1 medium sized onion, diced
- 1 large sized carrot, diced
- 1 celery rib, diced
- 1 garlic clove peeled and smashed
- 2 teaspoon of dried sage
- 1½ cup of bone broth
- 1 bay leaf
- 1 tablespoon tapioca starch

Directions

1. Pat your breast dry and season with pepper and salt

2. Melt butter in the instant pot while on Saute mode
3. Add the turkey breast and cook for 5 minutes until brown. Set aside
4. Add onion, celery, carrot to the pot and Saute for about 5 minutes
5. Stir in sage and garlic and Saute for 30 seconds
6. Stir in bay leaf, broth and scrape out the brown bits using a wooden spoon
7. Add the turkey with the skin side facing up
8. Close the lid and let it cook for 35 minutes at high pressure
9. Quick release the pressure once done
10. Transfer the breast to a carving plate and tent it with a foil
11. Allow to cool
12. Take an immersion blender and transfer the cooking liquid (from pot) alongside the vegetables and to a bowl and puree them until smooth
13. Return the mixture to the pot and allow to cook until it has thickened
14. Once done, slice up the turkey and serve with the gravy

Garlic and Port Wine Lamb Shanks

(Total Time: 30 Min|Serves: 2)

Ingredients

- 1 pound Lamb Shanks
- 1 tbsp Olive Oil
- ½ cup Chicken Broth
- ½ cup Port Wine
- 1 tsp Balsamic Vinegar

- 4 Garlic Cloves, minced
- 1 tbsp Tomato Paste
- 1 tbsp Butter
- ¼ tsp Thyme
- ¼ tsp Oregano

Directions

1. Heat the oil in your IP on SAUTE.
2. Add lamb and cook until browned on all sides. Transfer to a plate.
3. Add the garlic and cook for 1 minute.
4. Stir in the broth, port wine, tomato paste, oregano, and thyme.
5. Return the lamb shanks to the pot and close the lid.
6. Cook on HIGH for 17 minutes.
7. Stir in the butter and vinegar.

8. Serve the lamb topped with the sauce.

9. Enjoy!

Risotto with Shrimp and Eggs
(Total Time: 35 Min|Serves: 2)

Ingredients

- 1 cup Brown Rice
- 2 cups Water
- 1 Egg, beaten
- 1 ½ tbsp Sesame Oil
- ½ cup frozen Peas

- 2 tbsp Soy Sauce
- 6 ounces pre-cooked frozen Shrimp, thawed
- Pinch of Cayenne Pepper
- 1 tsp minced Garlic
- 1/3 cup chopped Onion

Directions

1. Heat some of the sesame oil in the IP and add the egg.
2. Scramble and cook until set. Transfer to a plate.
3. Heat the remaining oil and add onions and garlic and cook for 2-3 minutes.
4. Stir in the rest of the ingredients except the shrimp and egg.
5. Close the lid and cook on MANUAL for 15 minutes.
6. Do a quick pressure release and stir in the egg and shrimp.
7. Set to SAUTE and cook for 2 minutes with the lid off.
8. Serve and enjoy!

Provoking Goulash
(Total Time: 25Min|Serves: 6)

Ingredients

- 1-2 pound extra lean ground beef
- 3 teaspoons olive oil

- 1 large sized red bell pepper, stemmed and seeded (cut up into short strips)

- 1 large sized onion cut up into short strips
- 1 tablespoon of minced garlic
- 2 tablespoons of sweet paprika
- ½ a teaspoon of hot paprika
- 4 cups of beef stock
- 2 cans of petite diced tomatoes

Directions

1. Set your pot to Saute mode and add 2 teaspoons of olive oil
2. Add ground beef to the pot and cook as you stir until it breaks apart
3. Once the beef is browned, transfer it to a bowl
4. Cut the stem off the pepper and deseed them and cut into strips
5. Cut the onion into short strips as well
6. Add a teaspoon of olive oil to the pot alongside pepper and onion
7. Saute for 3-4 minutes
8. Add minced garlic, sweet paprika, hot paprika and cook for 2-3 minutes
9. Add beef stock alongside the tomatoes
10. Add ground beef
11. Allow it to cook for about 15 minutes on Soup mode over low pressure
12. Once done, quick release the pressure and have fun!

The "fall" Off The Bone Chicken

(Total Time: 29Min|Serves: 4)

Ingredients

- 1 whole piece organic chicken
- 1 tablespoon of organic extra virgin coconut oil
- 1 teaspoon paprika
- 1½ cups organic bone chicken broth
- 1 teaspoon of dried thyme
- ¼ teaspoon of freshly ground black pepper
- 2 tablespoon of lemon juice
- ½ a teaspoon of sea salt
- 6 cloves of peeled garlic

Directions

1. Using a small sized bowl, add thyme, paprika, salt and pepper and mix well
2. Season the chicken with the prepared mixture

3. Set your pot to Saute mode and add oil. Allow the oil to simmer
4. Add chicken making sure that the breast is facing downward and cook for about 6-7 minutes
5. Flip the chicken and pour broth, lemon juice and add the garlic cloves
6. Close the lid and cook on HIGH pressure for 25 minutes
7. Allow the pressure to release naturally
8. Transfer to your serving plate and allow to cool for about 5 minutes
9. Serve and enjoy!

Decisive Kalua Pork Meal

(Total Time: 105 Min|Serves: 8)

Ingredients

- 1 piece (4-5 pounds) of pork shoulder
- 1 tablespoon bacon fat
- 1 teaspoon of salt
- ½ cup diced pine apple
- 1 teaspoon fish sauce
- 1 tablespoon liquid smoke
- ½ cup water

Directions:

1. Set your pot to Saute mode
2. Cut the pork into two individual pieces and add the bacon fat to the pot
3. Add the shoulders and sear for about 2-3 minutes on each side to brown them
4. Sprinkle a bit of salt on top of the pork
5. Add fish sauce, pineapple, liquid smoke and water to the pot
6. Close the lid and cook for 90 minutes (over manual mode)
7. After 90 minutes, allow the pressure to release naturally for 10 minutes
8. Remove the pork from the pot and pour the juices into a jar
9. Take two forks and shred the pork
10. Add the juice to the pork and serve!

The Texan Beef Chili

(Total Time: 45 Min|Serves: 4)

Ingredients

- 1 pound grass-fed organic feed
- 1 sliced and seeded green bell pepper
- 1 large sized onion
- 4 large pieces of chopped small carrot
- ½ teaspoon ground black pepper
- 1 teaspoon sea salt
- 1 teaspoon onion powder
- 1 tablespoon chopped fresh parsley
- 1 tablespoon Worcestershire sauce
- 4 teaspoons chili powder
- 1 teaspoon paprika
- 1 teaspoon garlic powder
- Just a pinch of cumin

Directions:

1. Set your pot to Saute mode
2. Add ground beef to the pot and cook until it is nicely browned
3. Add the rest of the ingredients and give it a nice mix
4. Close the lid and cook for about 35 minutes over MEAT/STEW setting
5. Release the pressure naturally for 10 minutes
6. Open up the lid and serve. Enjoy!

The Excessively Juicy Apple Pork Tenderloins

(Total Time: 35 Min|Serves: 4)

Ingredients

- 2 tablespoons of clarified butter
- 3 pounds of boneless pork loin roast
- 1 large red onion halved and thinly sliced
- 2 medium sized tart green apples
- 4 fresh thyme sprigs
- 2 bay leaves
- ¼ cup of chicken broth
- ½ teaspoon of salt
- ½ teaspoon of ground black pepper

Directions:

1. Set your pot to Saute mode and heat up the clarified butter
2. Add tenderloin pieces, brown them for 8 minutes
3. Transfer them to another plate
4. Add onions and Saute for 3 minutes
5. Stir in thyme bay leaves, and apples

6. Pour broth and stir in salt and pepper
7. Nestle the pork loin in the apple mixture and pour juice from the plate to the pot
8. Close the lid and let it cook for about 30 minutes at high pressure
9. Release pressure quickly
10. Unlock and discard the bay leaves
11. Transfer the pork to a cutting board and let it cool for 5 minutes while you dish out the sauce into different serving bowls

Heartwarming Carne Guisada
(Total Time: 50 Min|Serves: 4)

Ingredients

- 2 tablespoons of avocado oil
- 1 pound beef, cubed
- 1 diced onion
- 1 ½ c. beef broth
- 1 tablespoon of minced garlic
- 1 Serrano pepper , minced
- 1 piece of bay leaf
- 1 teaspoon of ground cumin

- 1 teaspoon of chili powder
- 1 teaspoon of paprika
- 1 teaspoon of salt
- ½ teaspoon of pepper
- ½ teaspoon of oregano
- ½ a cup of tomato sauce
- 1 tablespoon of potato starch

Directions

1. Set your pot to Saute mode and add oil and beef cubes
2. Sear on all sides
3. Once the meat is browned, add onion, garlic, bay leaf, Serrano pepper and spice
4. Stir fry for 2-3 minutes
5. Pour beef broth and tomato sauce
6. Lock up the lid and cook on MEAT/STEW mode for 35 minutes
7. Once done, allow the pressure to naturally
8. Unlock the lid and remove it
9. Take a bowl and add potato flour and starch and stir to make a slurry

10. Add the slurry to the pot and stir well
11. Serve it over cauliflower rice
12. Enjoy!

Extremely Luxurious Rotisserie Chicken
(Total Time: 30Min|Serves: 6)

Ingredients

- 1 whole chicken
- 1 ½ teaspoon of salt
- 1 teaspoon of granulated garlic
- ½ teaspoon of pepper

- 1 ¾ tablespoon of avocado oil
- 1 yellow quartered onion
- 1 halved lemon
- 1 cup of chicken broth

Directions

1. Remove the chicken cavity parts and rinse them well
2. Pat your chicken dry with a paper towel
3. Take a small ramekin dish and add spices, pepper and salt
4. Add oil and give it a nice stir
5. Set your pot to Saute mode
6. Rub the breast with oil and the spice mix
7. Transfer the chicken breast to your pot and brown it for 3-4 minutes until fully crisp
8. Flip the breast and cook for 1 more minute
9. Add chicken stock and lock up the lid
10. Cook on HIGH pressure for 25 minutes and allow the pressure to release naturally
11. Remove the lid and transfer the chicken to your serving plate
12. Allow to cool for about 5 minutes and serve by pouring a bit of the cooking liquid

Orange Salmon
(Total Time: 25 Min|Serves: 4)

Ingredients

- 4 pieces of salmon fillets
- 1 cup of orange juice
- 2 tablespoons of cornstarch juice
- 1 teaspoon of grated orange peel
- 1 teaspoon of black pepper

Directions:

1. Add all of the listed ingredients to your pot
2. Lock up the lid and cook on HIGH pressure for 12 minutes
3. Allow the pressure to release naturally over 10 minutes
4. Open and enjoy!

Extremely Healthy Pineapple Pork Chop
(Total Time: 35 Min|Serves: 4)

Ingredients

- 6 pieces of thinly cut pork chops (bone-in)
- Balsamic glaze as needed
- Seasoning of your choice for the pork chops
- Olive oil as needed
- Cubed pineapple

Directions:

1. Season the chops well
2. Set your pot to Saute mode and drizzle olive oil
3. Allow the oil to heat up
4. Add pork chops and Saute well
5. Remove the chop and layer them on a steam rack
6. Glaze the top
7. Add pineapple chunks on top
8. Add a cup of water to the pot
9. Place the steamer rack on top of the pot
10. Lock up the lid and cook for 25 minutes on HIGH pressure
11. Release the pressure naturally and remove the chops
12. Serve with a bit of pineapple glaze

13. Enjoy!

Garlic-y Cuban Pork

(Total Time: 140 Min|Serves: 10)

Ingredients

- 3 pounds of boneless pork shoulder blade roast, fat trimmed and removed
- 6 pieces of garlic cloves
- 2/3 cup of grapefruit juice
- ½ a tablespoon of fresh oregano
- ½ a tablespoon of cumin
- Juice of 1 lime
- 1 tablespoon of kosher salt
- 1 piece of bay leaf
- Lime wedges as needed
- Chopped cilantro as needed
- Hot sauce as needed
- Salsa as needed

Directions:

1. Cut the pork chops in 4 individual pieces and add them to a bowl
2. Take a small sized blender and add garlic, grapefruit juice, lime, oregano, cumin, salt and blend well
3. Pour the marinade over your pork and allow it to sit for 60 minutes
4. Transfer the mixture to your cooker and add bay leaf
5. Cover and cook on HIGH pressure for 80 minutes
6. Release the pressure naturally
7. Remove the pork and shred it up
8. Return the pork back to the pot and add 1 cup of liquid
9. Season with some salt and allow to warm for a while (over Saute mode)
10. Enjoy!

Rosemary And Veal Stew

(Total Time: 35 Min|Serves: 4)

Ingredients

- 2 sprigs of fresh rosemary, chopped
- 1 tablespoon of olive oil

- 1 tablespoon of clarified butter
- 8 ounces shallots
- 2 chopped carrot
- 2 chopped stalks of celery
- 2 tablespoons of almond flour
- 3 pounds of veal, cubed
- Water
- 2 teaspoons of salt

Directions:

1. Set the pot to Saute mode and add olive oil. Allow the oil to heat
2. Once it is warm enough, add clarified butter alongside the chopped rosemary
3. Add shallots, celery, carrots and Saute until tender
4. Shove the veggies on the side and add the veal cubes
5. Brown them well
6. Pour stock and just cover the meat
7. Lock up the lid and cook on HIGH pressure for 20 minutes
8. Release the pressure naturally
9. Open up the lid and simmer for 5 minutes
10. Enjoy!

Chinese Beef Stew

(Total Time: 30 Min|Serves: 3)

Ingredients

- ½ pound beef cut into chunks
- 1 chopped small yellow onion
- 1 minced garlic clove
- 3 cups of beef broth
- 1 cup of sliced fresh mushroom
- ½ teaspoon of salt
- 1/8 teaspoon of black pepper
- 1 piece of bay leaf
- 1 fresh thyme sprig
- 1 tomato paste
- 1 tablespoon of Worcestershire sauce
- 1 tablespoon of chopped parsley

Directions:

1. Add all the listed ingredients to your pot
2. Lock up the lid and cook on HIGH pressure for 25 minutes
3. Release the pressure naturally
4. Open the lid and discard bay leaf, thyme sprig
5. Add some more salt and pepper if desired
6. Enjoy!

Meatloaf and BBQ Gravy

(Total Time: 34 Min|Serves: 4)

Ingredients

- 1 cup of canned crushed tomatoes
- ¾ cup of chicken broth
- 1 small sized sweet potato
- 2 tablespoons of date paste
- 1 tablespoon of vinegar
- 2 teaspoons of paprika
- 1 teaspoon of chili powder
- ½ teaspoon of ground cloves
- ½ teaspoon of celery seeds
- ½ teaspoon of salt
- 2 pounds of lean ground beef
- ½ cup of Italian seasoned dry breadcrumbs
- 1 large sized egg
- ¼ cup of loosely packed fresh parsley
- 1 tablespoon of Worcestershire sauce
- 2 teaspoons of minced up garlic

- 2 teaspoons of dried thyme

Directions:

1. Add broth, potato, vinegar, date paste, paprika, celery seeds, chili powder, cloves and ¼ teaspoon of salt
2. Keep stirring well
3. Add ground beef, parsley, egg, bread crumbs, Worcestershire sauce, thyme, ¼ teaspoon of salt in a large sized bowl
4. Mix well until the crumbs and herb have been distributed well
5. Place the mixture together to form a dome shape sphere and cut in half
6. Spoon in and smear some tomato sauce and set in the cooker mixture
7. Lock up the lid and let it cook for about 30 minutes at high pressure
8. Release the pressure naturally
9. Open up the lid and let it cool for about 5 minutes
10. Take it out and using a sharp knife, cut the meat loaf in ½ inch slices and serve in a plate
11. Dress it with a bit of sauce and serve

Original Bone-In Pork Chop

(Total Time: 26Min|Serves:4)

Ingredients

- 4 ¾ of thick bone-in pork chops
- Salt as required
- Ground Pepper as required
- ¼ cup of divided clarified butter
- 1 cup of baby carrots
- 1 chopped onion
- 1 cup of vegetables
- 3 tablespoons of Worcestershire sauce

Directions:

1. Take a bowl and add the pork chops, season well with pepper and salt
2. Take a skillet and place it over medium heat
3. Add 2 teaspoon of clarified butter and allow it to heat up
4. Add pork chops and brown them, each side should take 3-5 minutes

5. Transfer them to a plate
6. Add 2 tablespoon of clarified butter to your instant pot and set it to Saute mode
7. Add carrots and onion and Saute them
8. Pour broth and Worcestershire sauce
9. Add pork chops and lock up the lid
10. Cook for about 13 minutes at HIGH pressure
11. Release the pressure naturally
12. Enjoy!

An Awkward Garlic Potato
(Total Time: 10Min|Serves: 4)

Ingredients

- 4 medium sized russet yellow potatoes
- 1 cup of vegetable broth
- 6 cloves of garlic, peeled up and cut up into half
- ½ cup of almond milk
- Salt as needed
- ¼ cup of chopped parsley

Directions

1. Cut the potatoes into 8-12 chunks
2. Add them to your pot
3. Add broth and garlic
4. Lock up the lid and cook under HIGH pressure for 4 minutes
5. Release the pressure naturally
6. Mash the potatoes using a masher and add a bit of almond milk if needed
7. Stir well and serve hot!

Delicious Whole30 Sloppy Joe
(Total Time: 16 Min|Serves: 2)

Ingredients

- 2 tablespoons of olive oil
- 1 cup quinoa
- 1 large sized chopped yellow onion
- 1 large sized Italian frying pepper completely stemmed, chopped and deseeded
- 2 pounds of lean ground beef
- 2 teaspoons of minced up garlic
- 18 ounces crushed tomatoes
- ¼ cup of date paste
- 2 tablespoons of Dijon mustard
- 2 tablespoons of Worcestershire sauce
- 2 tablespoons of apple vinegar
- 2 tablespoons of paprika
- ¼ teaspoon of ground clove

Directions:

1. Open up your instant pot and toss in the grains
2. Pour in as much water, as required to cover up the grains
3. Lock up the lid and let it cook at high pressure for 3 minutes
4. Quick release the pressure
5. Open up and drain out the quinoa in a fine mesh sieve set in your sink
6. Heat up your cooker in sauté mode and pour some oil
7. Toss in the pepper, onion and cook for 4 minutes
8. Then, toss in the crumbled ground beef and garlic and keep stirring them nicely
9. Let it cook for 6 minutes until the beef is not pink anymore
10. Then, stir in the tomatoes, brown sugar, oats , mustard, vinegar, cloves, paprika and Worcestershire sauce alongside the nicely drained quinoa
11. Close up the lid and let it cook for 8 minutes at high pressure
12. Quick release the pressure
13. Open it up and serve hot

Crazy Lamb Spare Ribs (Overjoyed)

(Total Time: 320 Min|Serves: 5)

Ingredients

Ingredients for the Lamb

- 2.5 pounds of pastured lamb spare ribs
- 2 teaspoons of kosher salt
- 1 tablespoon of curry powder

Ingredients for the sauce

- 1 tablespoon of coconut oil
- 1 large sized coarsely chopped onion
- ½ pound of minced garlic
- 1 tablespoon of curry powder
- 1 tablespoon of kosher salt
- Juice of 1 lemon
- 1 ¼ cup of divided cilantro, chopped
- 4 thinly sliced scallions

Directions:

1. Take a bowl and add spare ribs
2. Season with 2 teaspoons of salt, 1 teaspoon of curry powder and mix well making sure that the ribs are coated fully
3. Cover it up and allow them to chill for 4 hours
4. Set your pot to Saute mode and add coconut oil
5. Add spare ribs and allow them to brown
6. Once done, transfer them to another plate
7. Take a blender and add tomatoes and onion and blend them well to a paste
8. Add the minced garlic to your instant pot (still in Saute mode)
9. Keep stirring the garlic while carefully poring the prepared paste
10. Add curry powder, chopped cilantro , salt and lemon juice
11. Allow the whole mixture to come to a boil
12. Add spare ribs and stir until it is coated well
13. Lock up the lid and cook for 20 minutes at HIGH pressure
14. Allow the pressure to release naturally once done
15. Scoop out the grease and season with some salt
16. Enjoy!

Amazing Lamb Stew

(Total Time: 55 Min|Serves: 6)

Ingredients

- 2 pounds of lamb stew meat cut into 1 inch cubes
- 1 acorn squash
- 3 large pieces of carrots
- 1 large sized yellow onion
- 2 sprigs of rosemary
- 1 bay leaf
- 6 cloves of sliced garlic
- 3 tablespoons of broth
- ¼-1/2 teaspoon of salt

Directions:

1. Peel the acorn squash and deseed
2. Cube the squash well
3. Slice up your carrots into circles
4. Peel the onion and cut it in half and slice the halves to make half moons
5. Add the ingredients (cut veggies and remaining ingredients) to your pot and cook on HIGH pressure for 35 minutes
6. Release the pressure naturally and enjoy!

Saffron and Pork Tenderloin Extreme

(Total Time: 15 Min|Serves: 4)

Ingredients

- 12 dried New Mexican red Chiles
- 3 tablespoons of steamed fresh thyme leaves
- 2 tablespoons of packed fresh chopped oregano leaves
- 2 tablespoons of smoked paprika
- 1 tablespoon of minced garlic
- ½ teaspoon of salt
- ½ teaspoon of saffron threads
- 3 tablespoons of olive oil
- 2 medium sized stemmed and cored, chopped medium green bell peppers
- One 2 ½ pound of boneless pork loin cut into ½ inch pieces
- 12 ounces drained and rinsed chickpeas
- 1 cup of chicken broth
- ½ cup of sherry vinegar

Directions:

1. Stem up and seed your chiles, tear them up into small sized bits
2. Place them in a medium sized bowl and cover with boiling water
3. Let soak for 20 minutes
4. Drain up the chiles into a colander and set in the sink
5. Transfer them to a blender and toss in the oregano, thyme, smoked paprika, salt, saffron and garlic
6. Cover and blend finely until smooth
7. Set your pot to Saute mode and toss in the bell peppers and cook for 3 minutes
8. Toss in the pork and stir it for 6 minutes until the color is lost
9. Lock up the lid and cook for 10 minutes at high pressure
10. Quick release the pressure
11. Unlock and serve

A Fine Looking Chili Chicken Verde

(Total Time: 50 Min|Serves: 4)

Ingredients

- ½ cup of water
- 3 pounds of skinless chicken breast
- ¾ pound of quartered tomatillos
- ¾ pound of poblano peppers with seeds and stems discarded
- ½ pound of Anaheim peppers with seeds and stems discarded
- 4-5 jalapeno peppers with stem removed and halved
- 1 quartered white onion
- 4-6 medium sized peeled whole garlic cloves
- 1 tablespoon of ground cumin
- ½ tablespoon of paprika
- 1 tablespoon of Kosher Salt
- 1 tablespoon of paprika
- 1 tablespoon of ground cumin
- 1 tablespoon of Red Boat fish sauce

Directions:

1. Add tomatillos, Anaheim pepper, jalapeno pepper, poblano pepper, garlic, cumin, onion, salt, paprika and chicken to the pot

2. Add enough water to cover it

3. Close the lid and cook on HIGH pressure for 25 minutes

4. Allow the pressure to release naturally and transfer the chicken to a plate and shred it

5. Add red boat fish sauce alongside the pot contents to a blender and blend well to form a nice puree

6. Serve the shredded chicken by pouring the sauce on top

7. If you want then you can wrap up the mixture in tortillas and serve as well with a garnish of shredded cheese

8. Enjoy!

Hearty Root Chili
(Total Time: 20 Min|Serves: 4)

Ingredients

- 10 ounces of sliced beets
- 1 cup of cooked ground beef
- 1 1/3 cup of diced carrot
- 1 1/3 cups of peeled and diced sweet potato
- 10 2/3 ounce of pumpkin
- 1 teaspoon of dried rosemary
- 1 teaspoon of sea salt
- 2 teaspoon of dried basil
- 2/3 teaspoon of cinnamon
- 13 1/3 of beef bone broth
- 1 1/3 tablespoon of Apple Cider Vinegar

Directions:

1. Add beets to a food processor and puree until smooth

2. Transfer the beets to the pot with remaining ingredients

3. Close the lid and cook on HIGH pressure for 10 minutes

4. Release pressure naturally and enjoy!

The Perfect Slider Meatballs For Your "Sliders"
(Total Time: 35 Min|Serves:6)

Ingredients

- 1 tablespoon clarified butter
- 40 frozen meatball
- 16 ounces marinara sauce
- 1 cup chicken broth
- ¼ cup fresh chopped basil

Directions

1. Set your pot to Saute mode and add melt the butter
2. Add meatballs and stir fry until browned (approximately 2 minutes)
3. Add sauce and chicken broth and mix well
4. Close the lid and cook on HIGH pressure for about 20 minutes
5. Release the pressure naturally over a period of 10 minutes
6. Allow it to stand for 5 minutes and stir in basil
7. Enjoy!

Happy Yet Spicy Picadillo
(Total Time: 20 Min|Serves: 6)

Ingredients

- 1 ½ pound lean ground beef
- ½ large sized chopped up onion
- 2 minced garlic cloves
- 1 chopped tomato
- 1 teaspoon kosher salt
- ½ finely chopped red bell pepper
- 2 tablespoons cilantro
- 4 ounces tomato sauce
- 1 teaspoon ground cumin
- 2 pieces bay leaf
- 2 tablespoons capers/ green olives

Directions:

1. Set your pot to Saute mode. Add meat and season with pepper and salt.
2. Heat as you stir until golden brown it
3. Add onion, garlic tomato, salt, cilantro, capers/olive, bay leaf, cumin, tomato sauce, water, pepper and stir for 1 minute
4. Close the lid and cook on HIGH pressure for 15 minutes
5. Release the pressure naturally and enjoy!

The Largely Skinny Steak Soup

(Total Time: 25 Min|Serves: 4)

Ingredients

- 1 pound diced steak, fat trimmed
- 1 large sized diced onion
- 2 large sized diced carrots
- 2 large sized stalk celery
- 4 pieces of sweet peppers diced up
- 8 ounces mushrooms
- 2 tablespoons garlic powder
- 1 tablespoon salt
- 2 tablespoons oregano
- 1 tablespoon thyme
- 1 piece bay leaf
- 1 cup crushed tomatoes
- 2 cups beef stock
- 2 cups water

Directions:

1. Set your pot to Saute mode and add stew meat
2. Brown the meat
3. Add onion, pepper, mushroom, carrots, celery and cook until tender
4. Add salt, spices, water and stock
5. Close the lid and cook on SOUP setting for 15 minutes
6. Release the pressure naturally and serve!

Life Altering Chicken Chili Verde 2

(Total Time: 25 Min|Serves: 4)

Ingredients

- 3 pounds bone-in Chicken Thighs
- 4-5 quartered tomatillos with husks discarded
- 3 pieces roughly chopped poblano peppers, deseeded and stem removed
- 2 Anaheim peppers roughly chopped, deseeded and stems removed
- 2 Jalapeno chilis roughly chopped with the stems and seeds discarded
- 1 medium sized onion
- 6 pieces peeled garlic cloves
- A bunch cilantro
- 1 tablespoon Fish Sauce

Directions:

1. Set the pot to Saute mode and add all of the listed ingredients
2. Saute for 3 minutes
3. Close the lid and cook on HIGH pressure for 15 minutes
4. Perform a quick release
5. Remove the chicken and shred it nicely
6. Blend the mix using an immersion blender
7. Season it well
8. Transfer the chicken back to the pot
9. Enjoy the Verde!

Very Subtle Balsamic and Cranberry Chicken

(Total Time: 40 Min|Serves: 4)

Ingredients

- 2 pounds chicken thigh skinless and boneless
- Salt as needed
- Pepper as needed
- 1 piece chopped red onion
- ¼ cup water
- 1 cup cranberry sauce
- 3 tablespoons balsamic vinegar

- 1 tablespoon Worcestershire sauce
- 1 tablespoon coconut aminos
- ½ tablespoon garlic powder
- ½ tablespoon rosemary
- 1 tablespoon cornstarch

Directions:

1. Spray your cooker with cooking spray
2. Set the pot to Saute mode and allow the oil to heat up
3. Season the thigh with pepper and salt and add them to the pot, making sure to brown them for about 4-5 minutes (cook in batches if needed)
4. Add chopped onion to the pot and Saute until slightly caramelized
5. Add water and scrape off the drippings
6. Using a mixing bowl, add cranberry sauce, balsamic vinegar, aminos, Worcestershire sauce, rosemary, garlic powder and mix well
7. Pour the sauce over the chicken thigh and mix well
8. Lock up the lid and cook for 15 minutes on HIGH pressure
9. Quick release the pressure
10. Remove the chicken thigh to your platter
11. Serve over noodles or rice
12. Enjoy!

Timmy's Pickled Green Chilies

(Total Time: 21Min|Serves: 1.5)

Ingredients

- 1 pound green chilies
- 1 ½ cups apple cider vinegar
- 1 teaspoon pickling salt
- 1 ½ teaspoon date paste
- ¼ teaspoon garlic powder

Directions

1. Add the above ingredients to your pot
2. Close the lid and cook under HIGH pressure for minute
3. Release the pressure naturally

4. Spoon the mixture into washed jars and cover the slices with a bit of the cooking liquid
5. Add some vinegar to submerge the chilly
6. Enjoy!

"Wow" Worthy Ghee Chicken

(Total Time: 32 Min|Serves: 4)

Ingredients

- 2-3 pounds boneless chicken thigh
- 1 tablespoon ghee
- 1 ½ large onion completely chopped
- 3 ½ teaspoon salt
- 2 teaspoon garlic powder
- 2 teaspoon of ginger powder
- 2 heaping teaspoons turmeric
- 1 ½ teaspoons cayenne powder
- 1 ½ cup stewed tomatoes
- 370 ml tomato paste
- 2 cans coconut milk
- 2 heaping teaspoons garam masala
- ½ cup slice almond
- ½ cup cilantro

Directions

1. Set your pot to Saute mode and add ghee, allow it to melt
2. Add 2 teaspoons of salt alongside onion and cook well
3. Add ginger, garlic, turmeric, coconut milk, canned tomatoes, paprika, cayenne pepper, chicken and mix well
4. Close the lid and cook on HIGH pressure for about 8 minutes
5. Once done, pour coconut cream, tomato paste and Garam Masala
6. Garnish with some cilantro and serve with a sprinkle of sliced up almonds
7. Enjoy!

Very Texan Stylized Beef

(Total Time: 45 Min|Serves: 6)

Ingredients

- 1 pound grass fed organic feed
- 1 sliced and seeded green bell pepper
- 1 large sized onion
- 4 large pieces chopped small carrot
- ½ teaspoon ground black pepper
- 1 teaspoon sea salt
- 1 teaspoon onion powder
- 1 tablespoon freshly chopped parsley
- 1 tablespoon Worcestershire sauce
- 4 teaspoons chili powder
- 1 teaspoon paprika
- 1 teaspoon garlic powder
- Just a pinch of cumin

Directions:

1. Set the Instant Pot to Sauté mode.
2. Toss in the ground beef and let it cook until it is brown
3. Toss in the rest of the ingredients and gently mix properly.
4. Close up the lid and press the warm button, after which press the meat/stew button
5. Cook for about 35 minutes keeping the steam valve closed
6. Once the timer runs out, naturally release the pressure out and serve

Feisty Sword Fish And Garlic

(Total Time: 190 Min|Serves: 6)

Ingredients

- 5 sword fish fillets
- ½ cup of melted clarified butter
- 6 chopped garlic cloves
- 1 tablespoon black pepper

Directions:

1. In a mixing bowl, add garlic, black pepper and clarified butter
2. Add cod fillet to a parchment paper and top with the garlic mixture and wrap up the fish
3. Cook for 2 ½ hours at high pressure
4. Release the pressure naturally

169

5. Serve and enjoy!

Crowd Favorite Lamb Shanks

(Total Time: 55 Min|Serves: 2)

Ingredients

- 3 pounds lamb shanks
- Amount of Kosher Salt
- Freshly ground portions of black pepper
- 2 tablespoons well divided ghee
- 2 roughly chopped medium sized carrots
- 2 celery roughly chopped celery stalks
- 1 roughly chopped large sized onion
- 1 tablespoon of tomato paste
- 3 cloves peeled and smashed garlic
- 1 cup bone broth
- 1 teaspoon Red Boast Fish Sauce
- 1 tablespoon vinegar

Directions

1. Season the shanks with salt and pepper
2. Melt a teaspoon of ghee in your Pot (Setting it to Saute mode) and add the shanks
3. Cook for about 8-10 minutes until a nice brown texture appears
4. Once the lamb is ready, remove it from the pot
5. Add the chopped veggies and a tablespoon of ghee and season with some salt and pepper
6. Once the veggies are ready, pour garlic clove, tomato paste and stir well for a minute
7. Add shanks, tomatoes, bone broth, fish sauce, pepper and vinegar to the veggie mix. Close the lid
8. Once the pressure is high, cook for 45 minutes
9. Once done, release the pressure naturally
10. Serve shanks and enjoy!

Very Friendly Ground Beef Chili

(Total Time: 50 Min|Serves: 10)

Ingredients

- 2 ½ pounds ground beef
- ½ of a large chopped onion
- 8 cloves of minced garlic
- 2 can of 15 ounce diced tomatoes
- 14 ounce can green chile
- 16 ounce can tomato paste
- 2 tablespoons of Worcestershire sauce
- ¼ cup chili powder
- 2 tablespoons cumin
- 1 tablespoon dried oregano
- 2 teaspoons sea salt
- 1 teaspoon of black pepper
- 1 medium sized bay leaf

Directions

1. Set your pot to Saute mode and add chopped onions
2. Cook for 5-7 minutes until translucent
3. Add garlic and cook for 1 minute
4. Add ground beef and cook for 10 minutes
5. Add remaining ingredients (except the bay leaf) and stir well
6. Close the lid of your pot and cook on MEAT/STEW setting for 35 minutes
7. Release the pressure naturally over 10 minutes
8. Discard the bay leaf and enjoy!

Chili Rubbed Salmon

(Total Time: 10 Min|Serves: 4)

Ingredients

- 1 pound salmon fillet cut up into 4 pieces
- Salt as needed
- Pepper as needed
- 3 tablespoons date paste
- 1 tablespoon chili powder
- 1 teaspoon ground cumin
- 1 teaspoon garlic powder
- 1 diced avocado
- 1 pint halved cherry tomatoes
- 1 teaspoon lime juice
- Chopped cilantro for garnish

Directions:

1. Add 1 cup of water to the pot and place a steam rack on top
2. In a small sized bowl, add cumin, garlic, and chili powder
3. Transfer the fish fillet to the rack and rub it well with the mixture
4. Close the lid and cook on HIGH pressure for 2 minutes
5. Release the pressure naturally and top with avocado
6. Enjoy!

Ultimate Corned Beef Brisket

(Total Time: 125 Min|Serves: 4)

Ingredients

- 1 piece corned beef brisket
- 4 cups water
- 1 small sized peeled and quartered onion
- 3 peeled and smashed garlic cloves
- 2 pieces bay leaves
- 3 whole sized black peppercorns
- ½ teaspoon allspice berries
- 1 teaspoon dried thyme
- 5 medium sized carrots
- 1 head cabbage, cut into wedges

Directions

1. Toss corned beef, onion, water, garlic cloves, allspice, peppercorn and thymes into your instant pot and close the lid and set the timer to 90 minutes
2. Release the pressure naturally.
3. Gently take out the meat and place them in a plate. Cover with a tin foil and let sit for 15 minutes
4. Toss in the carrots and cabbage to the pot and close the lid, letting it cook for 10 minutes
5. Once the cooking is done, release the pressure quickly and take out the prepared vegetables and serve them alongside the corned beef.

Yet Another Golden Age Bone Broth

(Total Time: 70 Min|Serves: 2)

Ingredients

- 1 cooked chicken carcass
- 1 inch knob ginger
- 1 small sized onion (quartered with the skin on)
- 1 cup chopped celery tops
- 2 tablespoons apple cider vinegar
- 3-4 liters water

Directions

1. Add all the above ingredients to your pot
2. Close the lid and cook for about 60 minutes at high pressure
3. Once done, allow the pressure to release naturally
4. Allow to cool for about 1 hour
5. Strain the solids into a large sized container and season the broth with some salt
6. Allow to chill overnight
7. Remove solidified fat from top and discard it
8. Portion it up and use accordingly

Easy To Make Belizean Chicken Stew

(Total Time: 30Min|Serves: 2)

Ingredients

- 4 pieces whole chicken
- 1 tablespoon coconut oil
- 2 tablespoons achiote seasoning
- 2 tablespoons white vinegar
- 3 tablespoons Worcestershire sauce
- 1 cup of sliced yellow onion
- 3 cloves sliced garlic
- 1 teaspoon ground cumin
- 1 teaspoon dried oregano
- ½ teaspoon ground black pepper
- 2 cups chicken stock

Directions

1. In a large sized bowl, mix achiote paste, vinegar, Worcestershire sauce, oregano, cumin and pepper
2. Add chicken pieces and rub the marinade all over them
3. Allow the chicken to sit overnight
4. Set your pot to Saute mode and add coconut oil
5. Once the oil is hot, add the chicken pieces to the pot and brown them in batches (each batch for 2 minutes)
6. Remove the seared chicken and transfer them to a plate
7. Add onions, garlic to the pot and Saute for 2-3 minutes
8. Add chicken pieces back to the pot
9. Pour chicken broth to the bowl with marinade and stir well
10. Add the mixture to the pot
11. Seal the lid and cook for about 20 minutes at high pressure
12. Once done, release the pressure naturally
13. Season with salt and serve!

The Zucchini Pesto Pasta

(Total Time: 13 Min|Serves:4-6)

Ingredients

- 1 tablespoon olive oil
- 1 roughly chopped onion
- 2 ½ pounds roughly chopped zucchini
- ½ cup water
- 1 ½ teaspoon salt
- 1 bunch basil leaves (picked off)
- 2 roughly minced garlic cloves
- 1 tablespoon extra virgin olive oil
- Extra zucchini for making Zoodles

Directions

1. Set your pot to Saute mode and add olive oil, allow the oil to heat up
2. Add onions and Saute for 4 minutes until translucent
3. Add salt, zucchini and water to the pot
4. Close the lid and cook on HIGH pressure for 3 minutes
5. Release the pressure naturally
6. Add basil leaves and garlic
7. Use and immersion blender to blend to a sauce-like consistency
8. Take some extra zucchini and pass them through a Spiralizer for noodle like shape
9. Toss the Zoodles with the sauce and enjoy!

Revolutionary Celery Soup

(Total Time: 40Min|Serves: 3)

Ingredients

- 1 large sized celery root chopped into 4-5 cups
- 1 medium sized chopped onion
- 4 peeled garlic cloves
- 3 cups vegetable broth (divided)
- 1/8 teaspoon white pepper
- ½ a teaspoon thyme
- ½ a teaspoon salt
- ¼ cup almond milk
- ½ teaspoon lemon juice

Directions

1. Set your Pot to Saute mode and add the onion and garlic. Heat until browning
2. Add celery roots and about 2 cups of broth
3. Close the lid and cook at high pressure for about 4 minutes
4. Let the pressure release naturally
5. Pour the cooked up celeriac and broth into a blender and blend until smooth
6. Pour it back to the pot and add white pepper, salt and thyme
7. Let simmer for 20 minutes
8. If soup gets too thick add some more broth
9. Add almond milk, pepper, salt, and lemon juice as well
10. Keep stirring it well and simmer for another 5 minutes
11. Serve hot

Very Enticing Lemon and Garlic Chicken
(Total Time: 40 Min|Serves: 4)

Ingredients

- 1 -2 pounds chicken breast
- 1 teaspoon sea salt
- 1 diced onion
- 1 tablespoon ghee
- 5 minced garlic cloves
- ½ cup organic chicken broth
- 1 teaspoon dried parsley
- 1 large lemon juice
- 3-4 teaspoons almond flour

Directions

1. Set your pot to Saute mode
2. Add diced onion and cooking fat and cook for 5-10 minutes.
3. Add the rest of the ingredients except arrowroot flour
4. Close the lid and set the pot to poultry mode
5. Cook until the timer runs out
6. Allow the pressure to release naturally
7. Once done, remove ¼ cup of the sauce from the pot and add arrowroot to make a slurry
8. Add the slurry to the pot to make the gravy thick
9. Keep stirring well

10. Serve!

The Perfect Mexican Beef

(Total Time: 45 Min|Serves: 4)

Ingredients

- 2 ½ pounds boneless beef short ribs
- 1 tablespoon of chili powder
- 1 ½ teaspoon of kosher salt
- 1 tablespoon of clarified butter
- 1 medium sized thinly sliced onions
- 1 tablespoon of tomato sauce
- 6 peeled and smashed garlic cloves
- ½ cup of roasted tomato salsa
- ½ cup of bone broth
- ½ teaspoon of red boat fish sauce
- Freshly ground black pepper
- ½ cup of minced cilantro
- 2 thinly sliced radishes

Directions:

1. In a large sized bowl, add cubed beef, chili powder, salt and give it a nice mix
2. Set your pot to Saute mode and add fat, allow it to melt
3. Add garlic and tomato paste and Saute for 30 seconds
4. Add seasoned beef, fish sauce, salsa and stock
5. Close the lid and cook on MEAT/STEW setting for 35 minutes
6. Release the pressure naturally and season with a bit of salt and pepper
7. Enjoy!

Simplest Meatball Ever

(Total Time: 30 Min|Serves: 4)

Ingredients

- 4 pound pork shoulder
- ¼ cup Jamaican jerk spice blend
- 1 tablespoon olive oil
- ½ cup beef broth

Directions

1. Rub the roast carefully with olive oil and coat well with the Jamaican spice mixture
2. Set your pot to Saute mode and transfer the meat to the pot, heat until browning
3. Add beef broth and close the lid, cook on HIGH pressure for 45 minutes
4. Release the pressure naturally and shred the meat
5. Serve and enjoy!

The Great Indian Goat Curry

(Total Time: 55 Min|Serves: 4)

Ingredients

- 2 tablespoons avocado oil
- 2 pounds goat meat
- 2 diced onions
- 1 ½ inch knob of fresh ginger, minced
- 3 minced cloves of garlic
- 1 bay leaf
- 4 whole cloves
- 4 cardamom pods
- 1 tablespoon coriander powder
- 1 teaspoon cumin powder
- 2 teaspoons salt
- 1 teaspoon turmeric powder
- 1 teaspoon Kashmiri chili powder
- 1 teaspoon paprika
- 2 cans organic diced tomatoes
- 1 teaspoon Garam masala
- ½ cup water
- ½ pound of potatoes cut up in half

Directions

1. Set your pot to Saute mode. Add oil and goat meat and allow to heat

2. Once the meat starts to brown, add onion, ginger, garlic, spices and bay leaf
3. Stir fry for about 2-3 minutes
4. Pour water alongside potatoes and diced tomatoes
5. Close the lid and cook on "MEAT/STEW" setting for 45 minutes
6. Release the pressure naturally and set your pot to SAUTE mode
7. Allow the stew to stay for a while if you wish for a thicker soup
8. Enjoy!

Italian Chicken Drumsticks

(Total Time: 30 Min|Serves: 4)

Ingredients

- 1 tablespoon coconut oil
- 1 ½ red onion, peeled up and halved cut up into wedges
- 1 ½ teaspoon salt
- 8 skin on chicken drumstick
- ½ teaspoon pepper
- ¼ teaspoon chili powder
- Just a handful of thyme sprigs
- Zest of ¼ lemon
- 8 cloves garlic
- 2/3 cup diced tinned tomatoes
- 2 tablespoons sweet balsamic vinegar

Directions

1. Set your pot to Saute mode. Add oil, onions, salt and cook for 2-3 minutes
2. Add chicken drumsticks and sprinkle a bit of salt, chili and pepper
3. Add thyme, tomatoes, balsamic vinegar, whole garlic cloves and lemon zest, give it a nice mix. Spread the mixture over the drumsticks
4. Close the lid and cook on HIGH pressure for 15 minutes (using the POULTRY settings)
5. Release the pressure naturally over 10 minutes
6. Serve over some veggies and enjoy!

Gluten Free "Glazed" Chicken Wings

(Total Time: 27Min|Serves: 4)

Ingredients

- 5 pounds chicken wings
- 1 cup hot sauce
- ¼ cup apple cider vinegar
- 1 tablespoon Cayenne pepper

- 1 tablespoon Ghee
- 1 teaspoon black pepper
- 1 teaspoon sea salt

For coating

- 1/2 cup of hot sauce
- 3 tablespoons Ghee

Directions

1. In a bowl, mix hot sauce, cayenne pepper, vinegar, black pepper, sea salt and ghee. Keep ¼ cup of the aside
2. Add the wings to your pot and pour the sauce. Mix well and cook for 10 minutes at HIGH pressure
3. Allow the pressure to release naturally over 10 minutes
4. Take out the wings and place them in a single layer on your cookie sheet
5. Baste the chicken with the sauce
6. Broil them in your oven for 1 minute
7. Once done, turn them over and broil for another minute
8. Make some extra sauce by mixing the ingredients (coating)
9. Baste the baked chicken with the sauce and coat them
10. Serve with celery sticks and carrots

Green Kale and Chicken Soup

(Total Time: 14 Min|Serves: 4)

Ingredients

- 2 tablespoons clarified butter/ghee
- 1 medium sized chopped up onion
- 3 peeled carrots cut up into bite sized portions
- 4 stalks of celery cut up into bite sized portions
- 2 bay leaves
- 1 teaspoon of salt
- ½ teaspoon of black pepper
- ½ teaspoon of dried thyme
- ¼ teaspoon of dried oregano
- 4 cups chicken broth
- 1 pound of shredded chicken breast
- 1 large sized handful of chopped up kale
- ½ teaspoon of fish sauce

Directions

1. Set your pot to Saute mode and add clarified butter, allow it to heat up
2. Add onion and Saute for 5 minutes
3. Add carrots, celery, bay leaves, thyme, salt oregano and pepper and saute for 1 minute
4. Add chicken broth and enough water to reach the 6 cup margin
5. Close the lid and cook on SOUP mode for 4 minutes
6. Release the pressure naturally
7. Allow the soup to rest for a minute and stir in fish sauce
8. Season with pepper and sauce and enjoy!

The Legendary Chicken Drumstick Soup

(Total Time: 30 Min|Serves:6)

Ingredients

- 1 ½ pounds chicken drumstick
- 2 large ribs of celery sliced up
- 2 medium sized peeled and diced carrots
- 1 large sized peeled and diced parsnips
- 1 medium sized peeled and diced rutabaga
- 1 small sized diced yellow onion
- 2 bay leaves
- ½ teaspoon of cracked black pepper
- 1 quart chicken broth

Directions

1. Layer all of the ingredients in your Instant Pot and top with the chicken broth
2. Set your pot to SOUP mode and allow it to cook until the timer runs out (default soup time)
3. Allow the pressure to release naturally over 10 minutes
4. Remove the meat from your drumstick and discard the bones, skin and cartilage
5. Return the meat to the pot alongside the remaining ingredients
6. Season well and give it a nice stir
7. Ladle the soup into serving bowls and enjoy!

Snuggly Pineapple Chicken
(Total Time: 50Min|Serves: 4)

Ingredients

- 3 pound of chicken breast
- 1 teaspoon of sea salt
- 4 slices of bacon
- 1 ½ cup of diced fresh pineapple
- 1 cup of diced yellow onion
- 2 tablespoons coconut aminos
- 3 ½ teaspoons Red Boat fish sauce
- 2 inch piece of peeled ginger root
- 4 minced garlic clove

Directions

1. Add chicken and sprinkle some salt
2. Add aminos, pineapple, fish sauce, onion and ginger
3. Close the lid and cook on HIGH pressure for 25 minutes
4. Release the pressure naturally over 10 minutes
5. Remove the chicken and transfer it to a bowl
6. Set the pot to Saute mode and add garlic alongside 1 ½ teaspoons of fish sauce
7. Simmer for 15 minutes until reduced
8. Shred the chicken and mix with the pineapple, bacon and onion
9. Top with the sauce. Enjoy!

Mocha Rubbed Delicious Pot Roast

(Total Time: 60 Min|Serves: 4)

Ingredients

For Mocha Rub

- 2 tablespoons finely ground coffee
- 2 tablespoons smoked paprika
- 1 tablespoon of freshly ground black pepper
- 1 tablespoon of cocoa powder
- 1 teaspoon of Aleppo pepper
- 1 teaspoon of chili powder
- 1 teaspoon of ground ginger
- 1 teaspoon of sea salt

For Roast

- 2 pounds beef chuck roast
- 1 cup of brewed coffee
- 1 cup of bone broth
- 1 chopped small onion
- 6 dried chopped figs
- 3 tablespoons balsamic vinegar
- Kosher salt
- Freshly ground black pepper

Directions

1. Take a small sized bowl and add the listed ingredients for mocha rub
2. Brew a cup of coffee accordingly
3. In a large sized bowl, mix beef cubes with 3 tablespoon of mocha rub
4. Add brewed coffee, broth, onion, balsamic vinegar, figs to a blender and blitz them to liquefy
5. Transfer the seasoned beef to your pot and pour the prepared sauce on top
6. Close the lid and press "Meat/Stew" button and cook them for about 35 minutes
7. Once done, release the pressure naturally
8. Open up the lid and transfer the beef to a serving platter
9. Shred with fork
10. Heat the sauce if you want it to be thicker and season accordingly
11. Pour the sauce on top of your beef and serve!

Pork and Napa Cabbage Soup

(Total Time: 60in|Serves: 4

Ingredients

- 1 teaspoon of ghee
- 1 small diced onion
- Kosher salt as needed
- 1 pound of ground pork
- 6 large sized shiitake mushrooms (stemmed and thinly sliced)
- 2 minced garlic cloves
- 6 cups of bone broth
- 1 head of Nappa cabbage (cut up crosswise into 1 inch segments)
- 2 large sized carrots peeled and cut up into 1 inch cubes
- Freshly ground black pepper
- 3 thinly sliced scallions

Directions

1. Set your pot to Saute mode. Add ghee, onion, salt and saute for minutes
2. Add ground pork and stir to break it up
3. Stir in sliced mushroom and additional salt
4. Cook for 5-7 minutes until no longer pink
5. Stir in minced garlic and cook for 30 seconds
6. Pour broth and bring the mix to a boil
7. Stir in carrots, potato and cabbage and bring the soup to a boil once more
8. Allow to simmer for 15 minutes
9. Close the lid and cook on HIGH pressure for 3-5 minutes
10. Do a quick release
11. Enjoy!

Chapter 4: Some Bonus Recipes

Compliant Mayonnaise Recipe

(Total Time: 10Min|Serves: 1)

Ingredients

- 1 whole egg
- ½ teaspoon of salt
- ½ teaspoon of ground mustard
- 1 ¼ cup of light tasting olive oil
- 1 tablespoon of lemon juice

Directions

1. Add egg, salt, olive oil and ground mustard to a bowl
2. Whirl the mixture in a food pressure for 3 minutes
3. Add lemon juice and pulse for a while more
4. Chill it in your fridge for 30 minutes
5. Store in a sealed container and use it with the recipes that need it!

Italian Dressing For The "Salads"

(Total Time: 4min|Serves: 1

Ingredients

- 1 tablespoon of chopped fresh herbs
- 1 teaspoon of dried oregano
- ½ teaspoon of sea salt
- ¼ cup of red wine vinegar
- ¾ cup of extra virgin olive oil
- ¼ teaspoon of freshly cracked black pepper

Directions

1. Add all of the listed ingredients to a tight fit jar and shake well
2. Taste it and adjust seasoning
3. Serve with salads!

Generous Balsamic Vinaigrette

(Total Time: 4Min|Serves: 2)

Ingredients

- 1 cup of extra virgin olive oil
- 1 tablespoon of Dijon mustard
- ½ teaspoon of Black pepper
- ½ teaspoon of salt
- ¼ cup of diced red onion
- 2 minced garlic cloves
- 3 tablespoons of balsamic vinegar

Directions

1. Blend all of the listed ingredients in a food processor until you have a smooth texture
2. Add a bit of olive oil to emulsify and use as needed

Delicious Spicy Buffalo Sauce
(Total Time: 10min | Serves: 0.5)

Ingredients

- ½ cup of Red Hot Sauce
- 2 ½ tablespoon of ghee
- 1 tablespoon of coconut aminos
- 1 tablespoon of apple cider vinegar
- ½ teaspoon of garlic powder
- ¼ teaspoon of cayenne pepper

Directions

1. Place a saucepan over medium heat
2. Add all of the listed ingredients and mix well
3. Once the ghee has melted, whisk well
4. Transfer the sauce to a glass jar and lock it up with lid
5. Use as needed!

Authentic Ketchup

(Total Time: 5min|Serves: 0.5)

Ingredients

- ½ cup of chopped pitted date
- 1 can of 6 ounce tomato paste
- 1 can of 14 ounce fire roasted chopped tomatoes
- 2 tablespoons of apple cider vinegar
- ½ cup of water
- 1 teaspoon of garlic powder
- 2 teaspoons of salt
- ¼ teaspoon of cayenne powder
- ¼ teaspoon of smoked paprika

Directions

1. Place a saucepan over medium heat
2. Add all of the ingredients and simmer for 20 minutes
3. Pour the mixture into your blender and blend until smooth
4. Season well and serve!

Delicious Tahini Sauce

(Total Time: 5 Min|Serves: 1)

Ingredients

- ¼ cup of tahini
- 1 tablespoon of apple cider vinegar
- 3 tablespoons of water
- ½ teaspoon of garlic powder
- Salt as needed
- Pepper as needed

Directions

1. In a small bowl, mix all the ingredients
2. Add a bit of water for a thinner sauce
3. Mix well and enjoy as needed!

INSTANT POT SNACKS AND APPETIZERS RECIPES

Chili Chicken Wings

(Total Time: 20 Min|Serves: 2)

Ingredients

- ½ tbsp. Sugar
- ¼ cup Butter
- 1 pound Chicken Wings
- ½ tbsp. Worcestershire Sauce
- 2 tbsps. Hot Sauce
- 6 ounces Water

Directions

1. Pour the water into the IP and lower the trivet.
2. Arrange the wings on the trivet and close the lid.
3. Close the lid and cook on HIGH for 5 minutes,
4. Do a quick pressure release.
5. Whisk together the remaining ingredients and brush over the wings.
6. Cook on SAUTE until sticky.
7. Serve and enjoy!

Boiled Peanuts

(Total Time: 80 Min|Serves: 2)

Ingredients

- 1 tsp. Cajun Seasoning
- 1/2 pound Raw Peanuts
- 2 tbsp. Salt

Directions

1. Clean the peanuts and place inside the Instant Pot.
2. Sprinkle with the spices and add enough water to cover them.
3. Close the lid and set the IP to MANUAL.
4. Cook for 70 minutes on HIGH.
5. Do a quick pressure release.
6. Serve and enjoy!

Swedish Party Meatballs

(Total Time: 20 Min|Serves: 2)

Ingredients

- 8 ounces cooked and frozen Swedish Meatballs
- 1 can Mushroom Soup
- ½ cup Sour Cream

Directions

1. Whisk together the mushroom soup and sour cream into the Instant Pot.
2. Place the meatballs inside and close the lid.
3. Set the Instant Pot to MANUAL.
4. Cook on HIGH for 10 minutes.
5. Do a natural pressure release.
6. Serve and enjoy!

Bacon-Wrapped Carrots

(Total Time: 25 Min|Serves: 2)

Ingredients

- 1/3 pound Carrots
- 3 ounces Bacon
- ¼ tsp. Paprika
- ¼ tsp. White Pepper
- 1 tbsp. Olive Oil
- ¼ cup Chicken Stock

Directions

1. Sprinkle the carrots with pepper and paprika.
2. Wrap them in bacon.
3. Heat the oil in your IP on SAUTE.
4. Cook the carrots until the bacon becomes crispy on all sides.
5. Pour the broth over and close the lid.
6. Cook on HIGH for 3 minutes.
7. Do a quick pressure release.
8. Serve and enjoy!

Scalloped Potatoes

(Total Time: 15 Min|Serves: 2)

Ingredients

- 2 Potatoes, sliced
- 2 tbsps. Sour Cream
- 2 tbsps. Milk
- 1 cup Chicken Broth
- 1 tbsp. Potato Starch
- ½ tbsp. chopped Chives
- ¼ tsp. Salt

Directions

1. Combine all of the ingredients in your Instant Pot/
2. Close the lid and set to MANUAL.
3. Cook the potatoes on HIGH for 5 minutes.
4. Do a quick pressure release.
5. Set the IP to SAUTE and cook for additional 2 minutes.
6. Serve and enjoy!

Buttery Lobster Tails

(Total Time: 25 Min|Serves: 2)

Ingredients

- 2 Lobster Tails
- 2 tbsps. Butter, melted
- ¼ cup White Wine
- ¾ cup Water

Directions

1. Cut the lobster tails in half and place in the steamer basket.
2. Mix water and wine in the Instant Pot and lower the basket.
3. Close the lid and set the pot to MANUAL.
4. Cook the lobster for 4 minutes on LOW.
5. Do a natural pressure release.
6. Drizzle with butter and serve.
7. Enjoy!

The Lifesaver BBQ Pressure Chicken Wings

(Total time: 10 minutes, servings: 8-10 wings)

Ingredients:

- 8-10 chicken wings,
- 2 teaspoons of olive oil,
- 4 drops of your favorite chicken wings.

Directions

1. Add your sauce to the chicken wings and make sure you marinate all over, then pour olive oil inside the sauce pan.
2. Pressure-cook the chicken for 10 minutes inside the olive oil, while the sauce pan is covered.
3. Pat the chicken wings dry, and serve.

The Instant pot Deviled eggs

(Total time: 30 minutes, servings: 12-16)

Ingredients:

- 6-8 eggs, boiled and peeled
- 1 cup (250 mls) of cold water,
- 1 tablespoon of extra virgin olive oil,
- 1 teaspoon of Dijon Mustard,
- 1 teaspoon of white vinegar,
- ½ teaspoon of Sriracha,
- 2 tablespoons of mayonnaise (full fat),
- ½ teaspoon each of ground black pepper and salt

Directions

1. Remove the egg yolks from the white eggs and gently smash the egg yolks with a fork and set the egg whites aside.
2. Make the dressing by adding the mayonnaise to the olive oil, Dijon mustard, white vinegar and Sriracha, and the mix into the smashed egg yolk.
3. Place the dressing inside a Ziploc bag and then cut a small corner with the aid of a scissors, before piping the dressing unto the egg whites.
4. Garnish your eggs by sprinkling the paprika unto the deviled eggs, and then season with the ground pepper and salt

Instant pot Korean Ribs

(Total time: 45 minutes, servings: 4)

Ingredients:

- 1 rack (2 lbs.) of back black ribs (kalbi marinade),
- 1 peeled and grated Asian pear,
- 1 whole minced garlic (37g),
- 1 minced small or medium onion ,
- ½ teaspoon of minced ginger,
- 1 teaspoon of freshly ground pepper,
- ½ cup of light soy sauce,
- 2 tablespoons of honey,
- 2 tablespoons of brown sugar,
- 2 tablespoons of unseasoned rice vinegar,
- 2 tablespoons of sesame oil
- 2 stalks of finely sliced green onions (for garnish),
- 1 tablespoon of toasted sesame seed

Directions

1. Make Kalbi marinade by mixing garlic, onion and Asian pear and process in a food processor. In a small bowl, mix the soy sauce, with honey, ground black pepper, brown sugar, rice vinegar and sesame oil, then add the mixture into the food processor to create a paste.
2. Marinate the baby back ribs by removing the outer membrane from the ribs, then place the ribs inside the Kalbi marinade inside a large Ziploc bag. Close the bag partially, then marinate the ribs inside the refrigerator for about 30 minutes.
3. Pour the Ziploc bag mixture into the IP and cook for 20 minutes.
4. Quick release the pressure. Brush the sides of the ribs and garnish with green onions and sesame seed before serving.

The Classic Instant pot Soy Sauce Eggs

(Total time: 20 minutes; Servings: 4-8)

Ingredients:

- 1 ½ cup of Chinese master stock (or Chinese marinade),
- 4-8 hard or soft boiled large eggs.

Directions

1. Place mater stock in the instant pot and bring to a boil for about 10 minutes. Perform a quick release once the cooking time is completed, and then open the lid gently. Pour the master stock inside a bowl and let it cool.
2. Add and eggs water in a steamer basket and pressure-cook for 5 minutes. Place the eggs in an ice bath for about 5 minutes and carefully remove the shells.
3. Infuse the flavor by placing the eggs into a warm bowl of the Chinese master stock, then cover before refrigerating for 2 hours.
4. Serve the eggs either cold or warm inside a sauce pan, after heating for a minute.

The Instant pot Chinese Braised Beef Shank

(Total time: 1 hour Servings: 4)

Ingredients

- 1 lb. (454g) of beef shank,
- 1 ½ (375ml) of Chinese master stock.

Directions:

1. Clean the beef by bringing about 1.5 liters of water to boil and then boil the beef shank for 3 minutes inside the instant pot.
2. Pressure-cook the beef by placing the ingredients inside the instant pot and then close the lid and set timer at 35 minutes press natural release after cooking.
3. Let the beef chill then submerge it in the master stock before chilling for 4 hours (or chill overnight).
4. Slice the beef thinly and garnish it with green onion before serving.

The Cheese Beer-Burger Dip

(Total time: 30 minutes, Servings: 4)

Ingredients:

- 1 cup of chopped mushroom,
- 1 finely diced large onion,
- 1 lb. of ground lean beef,
- 1/3 cup of beer (preferably, the Sierra Nevada Torpedo IPA),
- 1 teaspoon of salt,
- 1 teaspoon of garlic powder,
- 4 oz. of cream cheese(sliced into 8 pieces),
- 2 tablespoons olive oil
- 1 tablespoon of flour, and
- 1 cup of shredded sharp cheddar cheese.

Directions

1. Saute olive oil in the IP. Add the beef, onion and mushrooms and sauté for about 4 minutes until the onion become soften, and beef starts turning dark brown. Drain the excess grease from the beef mixture, and stir in the salt, beer and garlic powder. Cover and cook for 10 minutes at high pressure inside the instant pot.
2. Press the Quick release once the cooking time is completed. Stir in the cheese and flour. Return your instant pot and sauté for about 5 minutes until the dip becomes thickened and cheese is melted.
3. Serve immediately with corn dips.

The Buffalo Chicken Scalloped Potatoes

(Total Time: 20 minutes, Servings: 4)

Ingredients

- ½ cup of ranch dressing,
- ¼ cup of red hot sauce ,
- 8 red potatoes ,
- 2 cups of cooked shredded chicken,
- 2 cups of shredded sharp cheddar cheese.

Directions

1. Mix the ranch dressing with the hot sauce inside a bowl and then slice the red potatoes into ¼" thickness.
2. Pour ½ cup of water into the bottom of the instant pot, then layer the ingredients with the half of the potatoes at the bottom, followed with 2 tablespoons of the ranch sauce, half of the chicken , ½ of a cup of shredded cheese, and then repeat the layers once again. Cover the instant pot and set at high pressure for 5 minutes. Press the quick release once the cooking is done.
3. Transfer the potato mixture into a shallow baking dish. Top up with the remaining ranch dressing and the remaining shredded cheese. Broil inside the oven for 5 minutes until the cheese becomes bubbly and browned.
4. Serve immediately with the hot sauce.

The Steel Cut Oats

(Total time: 30 minutes, Servings: 2-4)

Ingredients:

- 1 cup of steel cut oats,
- 3 cups of water,

- 2 slices of apples or Cinnamon(toppings)

Directions

1. Combine the steel cut oats with water inside the instant pot, then seal the valves and set the timer at 3 minutes at high pressure.
2. Once cooking is completed, let it release its pressure naturally (this will take about 20 minutes). Serve the recipe with your preferred toppings

Instant pot Lentil Sloppy Joes

(Total time: 40 minutes, Servings: 2-3)

Ingredients:

- 2 peeled and diced carrots,
- 1 minced small onion,
- 2 cups of rinsed green lentils,
- 1 cup of water,
- 4 cups of pureed tomatoes (2 x 14.5 oz.),
- ½ cup of maple syrup,
- ¼ cup of apple cider vinegar,
- 2 teaspoons of salt,
- 2 teaspoons of cumin,
- 2 teaspoons of dry mustard,
- 2 teaspoons of garlic powder, and
- 1 teaspoon each of chili powder and paprika.

Directions

1. Mix all the ingredients inside the instant pot, then stir very well to blend and incorporate the flavor. Cover and cook for 20 minutes at high pressure. Let the pressure release naturally after cooking (this should take roughly 10 minutes).
2. Serve the lentil recipe with your homemade rolls, rice or potatoes.

Instant pot Avocado and Tunas Tapas

(Total time: 20 minutes, serving: 4)

Ingredients:

- 1 can (12 ounces) of packed white tuna – drained,
- 1 dash of balsamic vinegar,
- 1 tablespoon of mayonnaise,
- ½ teaspoon of black pepper (for added taste),
- 3 thinly sliced green onions, for garnishing,
- 1 pinch of salt,
- ½ chopped red bell pepper, and
- 2 ripe halved and pitted avocados.

Directions

1. In a medium bowl, mix the mayonnaise with the tuna, green onions, red pepper and balsamic vinegar. Season with garlic and salt.
2. Add avocado halves to the mixture.
3. Garnish with the green onions, and black pepper. Transfer to your instant pot and sauté at 15 minutes at high pressure. Then press the release manually.
4. Serve immediately.

Instant pot Espicanas con Garbanzos (Spinach with Garbanzos beans)

(Total time: 25 minutes, Servings: 4)

Ingredients:

- 1 tablespoon of extra virgin olive oil,
- 1 can of drained garbanzo beans,
- 4 cloves of minced garlic,
- ½ teaspoon of cumin,
- ½ of diced onion,
- ½ teaspoon of salt, and
- 1 box of frozen and chopped spinach (10 ounce of thawed and drained spinach).

Directions

1. Add olive oil to the Instant pot, and heat at high pressure. Add the garlic and onion and cook until they turn translucent (this should take about 5 minutes), with the sauté option.
2. Stir in your spinach, garbanzo beans, salt, and cumin, then use the stirring spoon to mash the beans as the mixture starts cooking (this should take about 15 minutes)
3. Press the pressure release and transfer into the serving bowl).

The Instant pot sautéed marinated shrimp

(Total time: 30 minutes, Servings: 6)

Ingredients:

- 1 cup of olive oil,
- 2 teaspoons of dried oregano,
- ¼ cup of fresh parsley (chopped),
- 1 teaspoon of salt,
- 1 juiced lemon,
- 1 teaspoon of ground black pepper,
- 2 tablespoons of hot pepper sauce,
- 2 pounds of large shrimps (peeled and de-veined with the tails still attached),
- 3 cloves of minced garlic,
- Skewers, and
- 1 tablespoon of tomato paste.

Directions

1. In a mixing bowl, mix the olive oil with the parsley, hot sauce, lemon juice, tomato paste, salt, black pepper, and oregano. Reserve a small amount for the basting that will be done later. Pour the remainder of the marinade into a big re-sealable plastic bag, alongside the shrimp, then seal and marinate the mixture inside the refrigerator for about 2 hours.
2. Turn on the instant pot and set the timer at 20 minutes and choose "sauté". Thread the shrimps onto the pot and pierce each near the tail and close to the head. Dispose the marinade.
3. Cook the shrimps for 10 minutes on each side until they turn opaque. Make sure you are basting frequently with the reserved marinade.
4. Once the cooking is completed, simply press the pressure release manually.

Instant pot Fig and Olive Tapenade

(Total time: 30 minutes, servings: 6)

Ingredients:

- 1 cup of chopped dried figs,
- ¼ teaspoon of Cayenne pepper,
- 2/3 cup of chopped olives,
- ½ cup of water,
- 1 tablespoon of olive oil,
- 2 cloves of minced garlic,
- 2 tablespoons of Balsamic vinegar,
- ½ teaspoon of salt,
- ½ teaspoon of pepper,
- 1 tablespoon of dried rosemary,
- 1/3 of chopped toasted walnuts,
- 1 teaspoon of dried thyme, and
- 1 package of cream cheese (8 ounce).

Directions:

1. In a pan, mix the figs with water and place over medium heat inside the instant pot. Set the option at "boil" at high pressure and set the timer at 20 minutes. Boil and make sure the fig become tender before reducing the liquid.
2. Press quick release and stir in your olive oil, rosemary, salt, pepper, Balsamic vinegar, cayenne pepper, and thyme. Refrigerate for about 4 hours to ensure the flavor blends very well.

3. Unwrap the cheese and place it on serving platter. Spoon the Tapenade prepared over the cheese, before sprinkling walnuts. Serve immediately with crackers or some slices of French brea

The Patatas Bravas

(Total time: 40 minutes, Servings: 2)

Ingredients:

- 2 russet potatoes (peeled, and sliced into 1-inch cubes),
- 1 clove of finely chopped garlic,
- 2 cups of olive oil,
- 1 minced red chile,
- 1 tablespoon of salt,
- ½ teaspoon of smoked paprika,
- 3 tablespoons of olive oil,
- 1 can of drained whole peeled tomatoes,
- 1 diced large onion,
- ¼ cup of mayonnaise, and
- 1 teaspoon of salt

Directions

1. In a large skillet, mix the potatoes, 2 cups of olive oil, and salt. Cook on high pressure for 25 minutes inside the instant pot until the potatoes are softened. Dry the potatoes until golden in colour (this should take about 6 minutes), then drain them on paper towels after frying.
2. Add 3 teaspoons of olive oil in a sauce pan. Add onions, salt, chile, garlic, tomatoes and smoked paprika. Simmer for 5 minutes.
3. Transfer the tomato mix into a blender, puree until the tomato sauce has become smooth.
4. Serve the Patatas Bravas with the tomato puree alongside the mayonnaise for dipping.

The Huevos Endiablados

(Total time: 25 minutes, Servings: 6)

Ingredients:

- 6 large eggs,
- 1 tablespoon of Dijon mustard,
- 1 can of tuna (4 ounces, drained and packed in oil),
- 1 teaspoon of garlic (minced),
- 2 tablespoons of diced red onion,
- ½ teaspoon of soaked paprika (you can have more for garnishing),
- 1 teaspoon of mayonnaise, and
- ¼ teaspoon of salt.

Directions

1. Place the eggs inside the instant pot and cover with sufficient water. Bring to a boil over at high heat, and press quick release before removing the boiled eggs. Let the eggs remain in hot water for about 15 minutes before you cool them under running water, and peel.

2. Slice each of the egg into half (lengthwise), and remove the yolks before placing them inside a bowl. Get the egg white on a platter, then mash the yolk alongside the tuna, mayonnaise, red onion, paprika, Dijon mustard, and salt, until the mixture becomes smooth and well combined. Fill each of the egg white half with a tablespoon of the filling, and garnish with remaining smoked paprika.

3. Serve immediately.

The Duck Bite

(Total time: 30 minutes, servings: 8)

Ingredients:

- ½ cup of dry sherry,
- 2 duck breast halves (skinned and boned),
- 1 tablespoon of soy sauce
- 16 drained whole water chestnuts,
- 1 tablespoon oil of peanut,
- 8 slices of halved bacon,
- 1 teaspoon of fresh ginger root (minced),

Directions

1. Whisk the sherry along with the ginger, and peanut oil, inside a mixing bowl, then cut the duck breast into 16 pieces and place them into the marinade alongside the water chestnut. Toss to coat. Set aside for about 5 minutes.

2. Set the instant pot at "sauté" option at high pressure, for 10 minutes.

3. Drain and discard the marinade of the duck breast, then place each piece on a water chestnut before wrapping it with a slice of bacon. Secure each wrap with a tooth pick before placing them into the instant pot. Repeat this step for the remaining ingredients.

4. sauté until the bacon has become crispy and turn once (10 minutes)

Instant pot Potato and Prosciutto Fritters (Polpette di Patate Fritte)

(Total time: 20 minutes, Servings: 4)

Ingredients:

- 2 large potatoes (peeled and coarsely shredded),
- 2 slices of chopped Prosciutto,
- ¼ cup of al purpose flour,
- ½ teaspoons each of ground black pepper and salt,
- 1 large egg, and
- 1 1/4 cup of extra virgin olive oil

Directions:

1. In a medium bowl, mix potatoes, flour, egg and the ham. Season with the salt and pepper, before forming fritters.

2. Heat oil in a sauce pan, then fry the fritters until they turn golden in colour (this should take about 5 minutes on both sides).

3. Press the quick release once frying is completed, then serve.

Instant pot Pipirrana (The Spanish Potato Salad)

(Total time: 35 minutes, servings: 6)

Ingredients:

- 6 large eggs,
- 1 can of drained Tuna (5 ounce),
- ½ cup of green olives with some anchovy or pimento (halved),
- 6 peeled and cubed potatoes,

- 1 green bell pepper (halved, diced and seeded),
- ¼ cup of extra virgin olive oil,
- 2 tablespoons of white vinegar (distilled),
- 1 red bell pepper (diced and seeded),
- ½ chopped large onion,
- 1 teaspoon of salt,
- 1 large chopped fresh tomato.

Directions:

1. Place the eggs in the instant pot and top with cold water before you bring the water to boil. Once boiled, remove from heat and allow to cool for about 12 minutes. Peel the eggs and cut them into quarters.
2. Boil a cup of salted water in the instant pot. Add the potatoes and cook until tender- this should take some 15 minutes. Drain the potatoes and transfer them unto a large bowl.
3. Toss the potatoes with the egg, and other ingredients, then refrigerate before serving cold.

Instant pot Gambas Pil-Pil (The Chilean Prawns)

(Total time: 20 minutes; Servings: 6)

Ingredients:

- 10 cloves of garlic (slightly crushed and peeled),
- 3 tablespoons of brandy or pisco,
- ½ teaspoon of salt,
- ½ cup of grapeseed oil or olive oil,
- 1 ½ lbs. of large shrimp (de-veined and peeled),
- ½ teaspoon of cayenne pepper
- 1 Cacho de Cabra pepper (or Anaheim pepper), it must be seeded and cut into ½ inch pieces, and
- 1 lime (cut into wedges)

Directions

1. Add garlic cloves and grapeseed oil to your instant pot, and cook for 10 minutes at high pressure. Cook until the garlic cloves turn golden brown, and the oil has become hot.
2. Add the shrimp and stir until well coated. Cook for about 15 seconds before stirring in your Chile pepper. Cook further until the shrimp has become firm

and pink. Pour in your Pisco, and cook for about 30 seconds until the alcohol has evaporated. Season with salt to taste, before pouring the mix into a serving plate. Serve the meal with sprinkled cayenne pepper and garnish with lime wedges.

Dessert recipes

The Instant pot Apple sauce

(Total time: 20 minutes, servings: 10)

Ingredients

- 6-8 large or medium size apples,
- 1 cup of clean water,
- 1-2 drops of essential oil (cinnamon), and
- 1 teaspoon of cinnamon (organic)

Directions

1. Cut the apples into chunks, and throw away the stems and seeds. Place them in instant pot along with water, and close the lid before setting the instant pot and cook for 8 minutes at manual high pressure. Make sure you seal the steam vent.
2. Allow the cooked apple sit for about 3 minutes, then turn the steam vent in order to release the pressure then open the lid.
3. Remove any excess water, and with the aid of electric mixer, smoothen the apple sauce to the desired consistency.

Instant Pot Apple Crisp

(Total time: 13 minutes serving: 1-2)

Ingredients

- 5 medium to large apples (peeled and chopped into chunks),
- 2 teaspoons of cinnamon,
- ½ teaspoon of nutmeg,
- ½ cup of water,
- 1 tablespoon of maple syrup,
- 4 tablespoons of butter,
- ¾ cup of rolled oats (old fashion),
- ¼ cup of flour,

- ¼ cup of brown sugar, and
- ½ teaspoon of salt.

Directions

1. Place the apples in the instant pot then sprinkle the cinnamon and nutmeg. Top up with the water and syrup.
2. In a bowl, melt the butter then mix with flour, oats, flour, salt, and brown sugar, then drop this mixture in spoonfuls, on the apples.
3. Secure the instant pot lid, then make use of the manual setting and set at high pressure with 8 minutes cooking time.
4. Make use of natural release and let crisp sit for about 3 minutes.
5. Serve while warm, and you can top up with vanilla ice cream.

Instant pot Apple Bread with Salted Caramel Icing
(Total time: 1 hour 10 minutes, servings: 2)

Ingredients :

- 3 cups of apple (peeled, cored and cubed),
- 1 cup of white sugar,
- 2 large eggs,
- 1 tablespoon of vanilla,
- 1 tablespoon of apple pie spice,
- 2 cups of flour,
- 1 stick of butter,
- 1 tablespoon of baking powder,

For topping, you need the following ingredients;

- 1 stick of butter,
- 2 cups of brown sugar,
- 1 cup of heavy cream, and
- 2 cups of powdered sugar.

Directions

1. In a bowl, simply mix the cream with the eggs, apple pie spice, butter and sugar until smooth and creamy. Stir in the apples. In a separate bowl, mix flour and baking powder and add to your wet mixture. Pour the batter in a pan and place on a trivet in your instant pot. Top with a cup of water and cook on high pressure for 70 minutes. Perform a quick release and then remove the top with the icing.

2. For the icing, simply melt the butter inside a small saucepan, then add the brown sugar and boil for about 3 minutes and until the sugar has melted. Stir in your heavy cream and continue cooking for about 3 minutes, until it becomes slightly thicken. Remove the saucepan from heat and let it cool before mixing in the powdered sugar and whisk until the creamy mix has no lump.

The Chocolate covered Strawberry Oats
(Total time: 14 minutes, Servings: 1)

Ingredients :

- ½ cup of strawberries,
- 1 tablespoon of mini chocolate chips,
- ¼ cup of boiling water,
- 1 cup of oats

Directions

1. Mix the strawberries with mini chocolate chips, then pour the water inside the instant pot. Set the timer at 10 minutes, at high pressure, then secure the valves tightly. Select "cook", and once the cooking time is completed, simply press pressure release.
2. Pour the thick and bubbly strawberry mix on your oats to coat and cool for 2 minutes to solidify.

The Toffee Almond Popcorn Balls
(Total time: 40 minutes, Servings: 16)

Ingredients:

- 2 tablespoons of unsalted butter (you may need more for shaping),
- 1 bag of miniature marshmallows (10 ounces),
- 16 cups of popped corns,
- ½ cup of toffee pieces,
- ½ cup of toasted almonds(chopped),
- ½ cup of miniature chocolate chips, and
- ½ teaspoon of coarse salt.

Directions

1. Melt butter in the instant pot. Add the marshmallows and cook further for about 6 minutes until it melts. Remove from heat and add the remaining ingredients. Once the cooking is done, simply press the pressure release manually.
2. Quickly, coat your hands with butter before shaping the popcorn mixture into balls. Place them on parchment lined baking sheet and let it cool for about 10 minutes before serving.

The Hard toffee

(Total time: 30 minutes, Servings: 14)

Ingredients:

- 1 cup of caster sugar (220g),
- 10g of butter,
- 2 tablespoons of boiling water ,
- 2 tablespoon of vinegar,
- 2 cups of crushed nuts

Directions

1. Turn on the Instant pot, mix all the ingredients (except the nuts), and heat on low heat until sugar dissolves, then bring to boil further for 15 minutes without stirring.
2. Pour the mixture inside the paper baking cases in patty pan hole before sprinkling the crushed nuts on top. Let set for about 10 minutes before you break into pieces and serve.

Peanut Butter Banana Oats

(Total time: 20 minutes, Servings: 2)

Ingredients

- ½ cup of chopped bananas,
- ½ cup of water
- 1 tablespoon of peanut butter,
- 2 tablespoons of honey or maple syrup , and
- 1 cup of oats.

Directions

1. Add all the ingredients (except the oats and honey) into the instant pot. Then press pressure cook, and set timer at 15 minutes. Once cooking is done, simply release the pressure manually and pour the paste-like solution on top of the cooked oatmeal.
2. Add the honey and stir to achieve a much better consistency.

Lemon Blueberry Oats
(Total time: 20 minutes serving: 2)

Ingredients

- 1 lemon (Zest and juice),
- ½ cup of blueberries,
- ½ cup of oats,
- ½ teaspoon of cornstarch.

Directions

1. Add the oatmeal into the instant pot with ½ cup of water and cook at high pressure for 10 minutes. While the oatmeal is cooking, simply place the blueberries in a saucepan, add 2 tablespoons of water, and sprinkle ½ a teaspoon of cornstarch. Stir the mixture and then bring to a boil.
2. Simmer the mixture and let thicken into a syrup-like substance. Once the oatmeal is done, simply stir and swirl in scoops of blueberry and serve.

The Sri Lankan style milk toffee
(Total time: 48 minutes , Servings: 25)

Ingredients:

- 2-4 teaspoons of butter,
- 1 ½ cup of white sugar,
- 3 tablespoons of water,
- 1 can of sweetened condensed milk (10 ounce),
- ½ cup of cashew nuts (finely chopped),
- 1 teaspoon of vanilla extract ,
- 2 drops of rose extract (for added taste)

Directions

1. In your instant pot, combine the sugar, butter, and water and heat at medium heat (cook and stir the mixture until the sugar dissolves). Pour in the condensed milk, then cook further until milk starts to generate bubbles (about 5 minutes). Reduce the heat to low and add the cashews before you cook further while stirring frequently until thickened (this should take roughly 10 minutes).

2. Stir in the remaining 2 tablespoons of butter, rose extract, and vanilla extract, then cook for about 10 minutes until the mixture becomes stiff. Pour the cooked mix into a pan, and with a spatula or back of spoon, simply spread evenly.

3. Cool the toffee trifle until it becomes firm (for about 15 minutes), cut them into 1-inch pieces before transferring into an air-tight container.

The Butter-Pecan Fudge

(Total time: 30 minutes, Servings: 64)

Ingredients:

- 1/2 cup of butter,
- ½ cup of brown sugar,
- ½ cup of white sugar,
- 1/8 teaspoon of salt,
- 1/2 cup whipping cream,
- 1 teaspoon of vanilla extract,
- 2 cup confectioners' sugar,
- 1 cup pelicans (chopped)

Directions

1. Combine all ingredients (except vanilla extract and confectioners' sugar), and bring to a boil inside the instant pot while stirring until the butter has melted and the sugar has dissolved. This should take some 5 minutes.

2. Remove from heat then add the vanilla extract and mix very well. Stir in the confectioners' sugar, until the mixture becomes smooth. Fold the pecans into a fudge.

3. Pour the fudge into a prepared pan and cool until firm (1-2 hours), then cut into 1-inch squares and serve.

Carrot cake Oats

(Total time: 20 minutes, Servings: 1-2)

Ingredients

- ½ cup of shredded carrots,
- 2 tablespoons of raisins,
- ¾ teaspoon of cinnamon ,
- ½ cup of oatmeal, and
- ¼ teaspoon of pumpkin pie spice.

Directions

1. In your instant pot, add oatmeal and ½ a cup of water and set at pressure cooking. Set timer at 10 minutes and secure the valves.
2. Add the cinnamon, shredded carrots and pumpkin pie spice and cook further for 5 minutes. Add the raisins to thicken the solution and let it cool until it becomes a cake.

The delicious family Almond Roca

(Total time: 25 minutes, Servings: 24)

Ingredients:

- 1 large grated and divided chocolate bar,
- 2 cups of white sugar,
- 1 lb. of butter,
- 1 pack of sliced almonds (divided and chopped).

Directions

1. Line a baking sheet with aluminum foil, then sprinkle ½ of the chocolate plus ½ of the almonds on the prepared baking sheet.
2. Turn on the instant pot and melt the sugar along with the butter over low heat. Increase the heat to medium and stir continuously until the mixture boils (20 minutes)
3. Pour the butter and sugar mix over the chocolate and almond on baking sheet. Sprinkle the remaining almond and chocolate over the butter and sugar mixture. Cool the mixture to room temperature, and refrigerate for about 1 hour before breaking them into pieces, and serve.

The Mason Jar Steel cut oats in Pressure cooke

(Total time: 25 minutes, servings: 1)

Ingredients :

- ½ cup of steel cut oats,
- 2 tablespoons of pure maple syrup,
- 2 tablespoons of chia seeds,
- ½ teaspoon of salt,
- ½ cup of extras (nuts, coconut, fresh or dried fruits, and spices),
- 1 cup of water (at room temperature).

Directions

1. Add the oats, chia seeds, syrup, salt, and extras into a pint-size mason jar, then add water (while leaving ½ an inch of head space). Shake until everything is well distributed and the chia seeds are not clumping together.

2. Place a small rack at the bottom of the instant pot and pour a cup of water into the pot. Choose "high pressure" and set timer at 20 minutes. Turn off the instant pot once cooking is completed, and make use of the natural release. Remove the lid once the valves have dropped.

3. Remove the jars from the pot and place them on cooling rack. Remove the lid of the jar carefully and stir the oats very well before topping up with a dollop of frozen whipped cream as garnish.

Coconut little kiss (Beijinho de coco)

(Total time: 40 minutes; Servings: 10)

Ingredients:

- 1 can of sweet, condensed milk (14 ounces),
- 1 tablespoon of butter ,
- Some sweetened coconut for decoration,
- Whole cloves for decoration, and
- ¼ cup of sweetened flaked coconut.

Directions

1. Simmer milk and butter in the instant pot. Cook and stir continuously, until the milk volume has been reduced to half and thickened (about 20 minutes).

Remove from heat, and stir in the coconut and allow to cool for 3 minutes before transferring to the bowl. Chill in refrigerator for about 2 hours.

2. With your oiled or buttered hand, form the milk mix into tablespoon-sized balls before rolling in the coconut flakes. Decorate each beijinho with a stick of clove.

Instant Pot Mini-Lemon Cheesecakes

(Total time: 18 minutes Servings: 6)

Ingredients:

- 6 half-pint mason jars,
- 16 oz. of cream cheese(at room temperature),
- ½ cup of sugar,
- 1 teaspoon of flour,
- ½ teaspoon of vanilla,
- ¼ cup of sour cream (at room temperature),
- 1 tablespoon of lemon juice,
- 1 lemon zest,
- 3 medium to large eggs,
- 1 jar of lemon curd,
- ½ cup of raspberries (optional), and
- 1 ½ cups of water.

Directions

1. In a large mixing bowl, mix beaten cream cheese with the sugar, and flour until creamy and no lumps. Stir in the vanilla, lemon juice, sour cream, and lemon zest. Beat in an egg at a timeuntil well-mixed (do not over-beat the eggs).

2. Fill each of the jar with ¼ of a cup of the batter of cheesecake, and then drop 1 tablespoon of lemon curd on top of the batter. Add an additional ¼ of a cup of cheesecake batter to each jar and on top of the lemon curd before you cover each jar loosely with foil.

3. Add the water to the bottom of the instant pot, and place the trivet at the bottom. Arrange 3 of the jars at the bottom of the instant pot, and then stark the remaining 3 jars on top of the first three. Secure the instant pot lid and ensure that the vent remains in the pressure cooking point.

211

4. Set timer at 8 minutes and manually cook. Once the cooking is completed, simply perform a manual pressure release and carefully remove the jars from the instant pot with the aid of a pad or towel. Cool the cheesecakes at room temperature until they are ready to be served.

5. Garnish the cheesecakes with raspberries and additional lemon curds.

The Knack toffee

(Total time: 45 minutes, Servings: 48)

Ingredients:

- ¾ cup of light molasses,
- ¾ cup of heavy whipping cream,
- 2 teaspoons of cocoa powder (unsweetened),
- ¼ cup of chopped almonds,
- 1 teaspoon of vanilla extract, and
- ¾ cup of white sugar.

Directions

1. Mix all the ingredients (except vanilla extract and almond), inside the instant pot and bring the mixture to a boil (20 minutes). Stir in the vanilla and almond.

2. Spoon the candy into some small paper candy cups, then cool it to room temperature before you store in air-tight container at room temperature.

Instant pot Homemade Pumpkin puree

(Total time: 30 minutes, serving: 2-3)

Ingredient :

- 4 lbs. of pie pumpkin,
- 1 cup of water.

Directions

1. Remove stems from pumpkin. Place the rack of steamer basket at the bottom of the instant pot and add water. Place your pumpkin on the rack of basket,

and make sure the lid of the instant pot can be closed without it touching the top of the pumpkin.

2. Seal your instant pot and cook the pumpkin for 13 minutes, then let the pressure release itself naturally. Gently lift the pumpkin out of the pressure cooker before placing it on a cutting board or plate and let cool for about 2 minutes.

3. Slice the pumpkin in halves and then remove the seeds before you goop and peel the skin.

4. Blend the pumpkin inside a blender or food processor, and add a tablespoon of water. Make sure it is smooth after blending.

5. Store it in the refrigerator until needed.

The four-ingredient toffee
(Total time: 30 minutes, Servings: 36)

Ingredients:

- 1 cup of sugar,
- 1 cup of butter or margarine,
- ½ cup of semi-sweet chocolate chips,
- ½ cup of finely chopped pecans, and
- ¼ cup of water.

Directions

1. In your Instant pot, add butter, water, and sugar and bring to a boil as you stir. Reduce heat to medium and cook for 10 minutes.

2. Pour the toffee immediately into an ungreased cooking sheet, and spread it into ¼ inch thickness. Sprinkle the chocolate chips and let the mixture stand for about 1 minute or until the chips become softened. Spread the softened chocolate evenly on the toffee before you sprinkle the pecans.

3. Let the toffee stand under room temperature for about 20 minutes until firm. Break them into bite sizes and serve or store in refrigerator.

Lia's butter toffee
(Total time: 40 minutes, Servings: 18)

Ingredients:

- 16 ounces of melted butter,
- 16 ounce of granulated sugar,
- 3 ounces of water,
- 1 teaspoon of salt,
- 1 teaspoon of vanilla extract,
- 16 ounces mix of toppings (toasted nuts, sea salt, and candy canes), and
- 24 ounces of tempered dark chocolate (melted) - for coating.

Directions

1. In your instant pot, mix the butter with the sugar, and water and bring to boil while stirring constantly (5 minutes)
2. Remove the mixture from heat before adding the vanilla and combine very well. Pour the mixture into a silicone baking mat or a parchment paper. Make use of a spatula to spread the toffee quickly before it sets. Spread the toffee evenly and allow to cool and blot to remove excess oil at the surface. Coat the surface with half of the melted chocolate and sprinkle with the topping.
3. Once the chocolate has set, flip over and coat the other side with the remaining chocolate. Sprinkle the remaining toppings. Allow to set before breaking into pieces, and serve.

The white chocolate coffee toffee
(Total time 40 minutes, Servings: 15)

Ingredients:

- 8 ounces of white chopped chocolate,
- ½ cup of toffee baking bits,
- 1/3 cup of chocolate –covered toffee bits and
- 2 teaspoons of coffee beans (finely grounded).

Directions

1. Butter a single baking sheet and line it with waxed paper.
2. Melt the chocolate inside the instant pot for 10 minutes at high temperature, as you stir frequently while scrapping down the sides with a spatula to prevent

scorching. Stir in other ingredients and cook for 10 minutes before removing from heat. Spread the mixture unto a prepared baking dish, then refrigerate until it becomes hardened. Break them into pieces and serve.

Mini Turkey Bites

(Total Time: 20 Min|Serves: 2)

Ingredients

- 1/3 pound ground Turkey
- 1 small Egg
- 1 ½ cups Chicken Broth
- ¼ cup Breadcrumbs
- 1 tbsp Olive Oil
- ½ tbsp chopped Parsley
- Pinch of Garlic Powder
- Pinch of Paprika

Directions

1. Combine turkey, parsley, garlic, breadcrumbs, egg, and paprika, in a bowl.
2. Shape into bite-sized pieces.
3. Heat the oil in the IP and place the bites in it.
4. Cook until browned on all sides.
5. Pour the broth over and close the lid.
6. Cook the bites for about 5 minutes on HIGH.
7. Do a quick pressure release.
8. Serve with your favorite sauce and enjoy!

Spicy Corn Cob

(Total Time: 10 Min|Serves: 2)

Ingredients

- 1 ½ cups Water
- 2 Ears of Corn
- 2 tsps. Butter
- ½ tbsp Chili Powder
- ¼ tsp Cayenne Pepper
- ¼ tsp Paprika
- ¼ tsp Salt

Directions

1. Pour the water into the IP and lower the rack.

2. Arrange the corn on the rack and close the lid.
3. Cook on HIGH for 3 minutes.
4. Do a quick pressure release.
5. Top with butter and sprinkle the spices over.
6. Serve and enjoy!

Garlic and Butter Crab Legs
(Total Time: 10 Min|Serves: 2)

Ingredients

- ½ pounds Carrots, sliced into sticks
- ¼ tsp Cinnamon
- 1 tbsp Agave Nectar
- 2 tbsp Butter
- Pinch of Salt
- 1 ½ cups Water

Directions

1. Pour the water into the IP and lower the rack.
2. Arrange the carrots on the rack and close the lid.
3. Cook on STEAM for 4 minutes.
4. Do a quick pressure release.
5. Whisk together the agave, butter, salt, and cinnamon.
6. Brush this mixture over the carrots.
7. Serve the sticks with your favorite sauce or hummus, and enjoy.

Instant Eggplant Dip
(Total Time: 10 Min|Serves: 2)

Ingredients

- ½ Eggplant, diced
- 1 tbsp chopped Cilantro
- 1 tbsp Oil
- ¾ cup Water
- ½ tsp minced Garlic
- ½ tbsp Sesame Paste
- ¼ tsp Pepper
- ¼ tsp Salt

Directions

1. Place the eggplants and water in the IP and close the lid.

2. Cook on STEAM for 10 minutes.
3. Do a quick pressure release, drain and transfer to a food processor.
4. Add the rest of the ingredients and pulse until smooth.
5. Serve and enjoy!

Kale Tahini Hummus

(Total Time: 25 Min|Serves: 2)

Ingredients

- ½ cup Chickpeas
- 1 tbsp Tahini
- ½ cup chopped Kale
- 1 ½ cups Water
- ¼ cup minced Green Onions
- ½ tbsp Olive Oil
- Salt and Pepper, to taste

Directions

1. Place the water and chickpeas inside the IP and close the lid.
2. Cook on BEANS/CHILI for 15 minutes.
3. Do a quick pressure release.
4. Transfer the chickpeas along with the other ingredients to a food processor.
5. Pulse until smooth.
6. Serve as desired and enjoy!

Veggie Cheesy Appetizer

(Total Time: 25 Min|Serves: 2)

Ingredients

- ½ cup grated Cheddar Cheese
- 1/3 cup Broccoli Florets
- ¼ cup Ricotta Cheese
- ½ pound Potatoes, diced
- ¼ cup chopped Carrots
- ¼ tsp Cumin
- ¼ tsp Cayenne Pepper
- Salt and Pepper, to taste
- 1 tbsp Olive Oil
- 1 ½ cups Water

Directions

1. Combine the veggies and water in the IP and close the lid.
2. Cook on MANUAL for 12 minutes.
3. Do a quick pressure release.
4. Drain and transfer to a bowl.
5. Stir in the remaining ingredients.

Serve and enjoy!

36 Months Instant pot Meal Plan

	Menu for month 1			
	week 1	week 2	week 3	week 4
Mon	Protein Packed "Cakes"	Breakfast Cinnamon Bread	Spicy Shrimp and Tomato Casserole	Provoking Goulash
Tues	Southern Breakfast Cornbread	Authentic Shredded Chicken	Turkey with Cranberries and Sauerkraut	The "fall" Off The Bone Chicken
Wed	Corned Beef with Potatoes and Red Cabbage	Creamy Herbed Eggs	Lettuce Wrap "Taco" Chicken	Decisive Kalua Pork Meal
Thu	Mashed Cauliflower and Potatoes	The "Squash" Spaghetti	Delicious Prosciutto Wrapped Cane	The Texan Beef Chili
Fri	Simple "Hard" Boiled Eggs	Brown Sugar and Soy Short Ribs	Refreshing Turkey Meal	Chili Chicken Wings
Sat	Very Friendly Egg Roll Soup	Fine Fennel Shredded Chicken	Garlic and Port Wine Lamb Shanks	Boiled Peanuts
Sun	A Chicken "Faux" Pho	Cheesy Pepperoni and Spinach Frittata	Risotto with Shrimp and Eggs	Swedish Party Meatballs

	Menu for month 2			
	week 1	week 2	week 3	week 4
Mon	Bacon-Wrapped Carrots	Mexican Rice Casserole	Flavorful Bone Broth	Supremely Spicy And Ravaging Chicken Stew
Tues	Breakfast Cinnamon Bread	Scalloped Potatoes	Pasta Bolognese	Heartwarming Spaghetti Squash and Chicken Marsala
Wed	The Excessively Juicy Apple Pork Tenderloins	Simplest Meatball Ever	Buttery Lobster Tails	A Very Orange Salmon
Thu	Heartwarming Carne Guisada	Extremely Luxurious Rotisserie Chicken	Butternut Squash Soup	Mini Turkey Bites

219

Fri	Extremely Healthy Pineapple Pork Chop	Garlic-y Cuban Pork	Compliant Mayonnaise Recipe	Instant Scotch Eggs
Sat	Italian Dressing For The "Salads"	Generous Balsamic Vinaigrette	Delicious Spicy Buffalo Sauce	Authentic Ketchup
Sun	Delicious Tahini Sauce	Spicy Corn Cob	Garlic and Butter Crab Legs	Agave Carrot Sticks

Menu for month 3				
	week 1	week 2	week 3	week 4
Mon	Blueberry Cheesecake Pancake	Thyme and Rosemary Lambs with Carrots	Rosemary And Veal Stew	A Very Chinese Beef Stew
Tues	The Instant Pulled Pork Ragu	Mind-Blowing Brussels	Chili Chicken Curry	All Natural "Sugar" Free Applesauce
Wed	Blessed Ligurian Chicken	Instant Eggplant Dip	Lemony Tapioca Pearls	Veggie Cheesy Appetizer
Thu	Amazing Lamb Stew	Amazing Beef Short Ribs	Kale Tahini Hummus	Beef and Mushroom Stew
Fri	Simple Instant Hardboiled Eggs	An Awkward Garlic Potato	Crazy Lamb Spare Ribs (Overjoyed)	Delicious Whole30 Sloppy Joe
Sat	Fish and Potatoes Packet	A Rough Patch Potato Roast	Cheddar and Bean Quessadillas	Kale and Spinach Risotto
Sun	Original Bone-In Pork Chop	Instant Halved Chicken	Meatloaf and BBQ Gravy	Cheesy Breakfast Bagels

Menu for month 4				
	week 1	week 2	week 3	week 4
Mon	Very Fresh Pinna Colada Chicken!	Lightly Appetizing Chicken Balls	Mushroom and Onion Egg Cups	Carrot and Spinach Sausage-Crusted Quiche
Tues	Bacon Thyme Eggs	Blueberry Coconut Porridge	Sassy Spaghetti Squash With Garlic and Sage	Lovely And Healthy Beets

Wed	Thick Pork Chops With Artichoke and Lemon	Mexican Chicken Cacciatore	Lobster and Cheese Pasta	Juicy and Tender Chicken Drumsticks
Thu	Caribbean Beef	Broccoli Soup With The Blessing Of The Divine	Amazing Pork Chop Of Ghee	Tender Soft Daikon Noodles
Fri	Beef Tips in Sauce with Rice	Tomato Tuna Pasta with Capers	Saffron and Pork Tenderloin Extreme	A Fine Looking Chili Chicken Verde
Sat	Hearty Root Chili	The Perfect Slider Meatballs For Your "Sliders"	Happy Yet Spicy Picadillo	The Largely Skinny Steak Soup
Sun	Instant Eggplant Dip	Kale Tahini Hummus	Veggie Cheesy Appetizer	Life Altering Chicken Chili Verde 2

Menu for month 5				
	week 1	week 2	week 3	week 4
Mon	Garden Quiche	The Very Curious Zuppa Toscana	Very Yummy Chicken Yum Yum (Whole30)	Lemony Salmon
Tues	Pulled Apart Pork Carnitas	Jalapeno Egg Poppers	Very Subtle Balsamic and Cranberry Chicken	The Authentic Roast and Veggies
Wed	Goose with Apples and Raisins	Pork Chops with Apples	Turmeric Diced Eggs	Life Altering Chicken Chili Verde 2
Thu	Absolutely Incredible Asparagus Soup	Timmy's Pickled Green Chilies	Acorn Squash With Pork Chops	A Delightful Picnic Salad
Fri	Rich Fish Stew	Sausage, Tomato & Corn Breakfast	Amazing Beef Bourguignon	"Wow" Worthy Ghee Chicken
Sat	Astonishing Cauliflower Rice	Buffalo Chicken and Potatoes	Classic Cornmeal in the Instant Pot	Very Curious Vietnamese Bo Kho
Sun	Classic Mac and Cheese	The Less "Stinky" Onion Soup	Pulled Pork with Cranberries	Espresso Oatmeal

	week 1	week 2	week 3	week 4
			Menu for month 6	
Mon	Great Morning Guacamole As A Spread	Cheesy Breakfast Steak Rolls	Instant Breakfast Bread	Multi-Grain Breakfast Porridge
Tues	The "Stinking Rose"	Mashed Assorted Selected Of Veggies	Your New Breakfast Pal "The Boiled Egg"	Spicy Monterey Jack Omelet
Wed	Innocent Korean Short Ribs	Life Altering Chicken Chili Verde 2	Very Subtle Balsamic and Cranberry Chicken	Timmy's Pickled Green Chilies
Thu	Feisty Sword Fish And Garlic	Steak with Veggies	"Wow" Worthy Ghee Chicken	Very Texan Stylized Beef
Fri	Sweet Pineapple Glazed Ham	Crowd Favorite Lamb Shanks	Cordon Bleu Pasta	
Sat	Ultimate Corned Beef Brisket	Gentle Giant's Beef Stroganoff	Very Friendly Ground Beef Chili	Herb-Loaded Instant Meatloaf
Sun	Smothered Barbecue Ribs with Cinnamon	Yet Another Golden Age Bone Broth	The Perfect English Stew	Chili Rubbed Salmon

	week 1	week 2	week 3	week 4
			Menu for month 7	
Mon	Instant Breakfast Burrito	Easy To Make Belizean Chicken Stew	Taco Pie	The Zucchini Pesto Pasta
Tues	Revolutionary Celery Soup	Eggs and Smoked Salmon	Very Enticing Lemon and Garlic Chicken	Tuna Noodles with Peas and Cheese
Wed	Sausage and Ham Omelet	The Perfect Mexican Beef	An Old Fashioned Baked Potato	The Great Indian Goat Curry
Thu	Chili Lime Chicken with Rice	Juicy Apple and Cherry Breakfast Rice Pudding	Simplest Meatball Ever	Eggplant Olive Spread For Generations To Come
Fri	Vegetarian Burger Pattis	Spaghetti Squash "Cooked"	Mesmerizing Piccata Potatoes	Italian Chicken Drumsticks

222

Sat	Tre Colore Frittata	Tilapia and Tomatoes	Extremely Juicy Apple BBQ Ribs	Pear and Pork Loin Chops
Sun	Gluten Free "Glazed" Chicken Wings	Eggplant Tahini Toast with Olives	The Supreme Pork Shoulder	Astonishing Vegetable Chicken Breast

Menu for month 8				
	week 1	week 2	week 3	week 4
Mon	Pumpkin Pie Oatmeal	Mesmerizing Braised Kale and Carrots	Green Kale and Chicken Soup	Snuggly Pineapple Chicken
Tues	The Legendary Chicken Drumstick Soup	Heart Warming Baby Carrots	Chard and Mushroom Risotto	Beef Bourguignon
Wed	Chorizo Pepper Jack Frittata	Asian Salmon And Veggies	A Gentle Early Morning Carrot Soup	Ever So Brilliant Mango Chicken
Thu	Mocha Rubbed Delicious Pot Roast	Supreme Celery and Potato Soup	Pork and Napa Cabbage Soup	Crustless Kale and Tomato Quiche
Fri	Feta and Leafy Green Egg Cups	Pastrami from the Instant Pot	The Best "Steamed" Chokes	Instant Lasagna
Sat	Ketchup Glazed Pork Meatloaf	Sautéed Mushrooms For A Healthy Morning	A Salsa Chicken Full Of Magic	Almond and Apricot Oatmeal
Sun	A Happy Morning's Picnic Salad	Compliant Mayonnaise Recipe	Early Bird Egg Roll Bowl	Italian Dressing For The "Salads"

Menu for month 9				
	week 1	week 2	week 3	week 4
Mon	Prosciutto Mozzarella Egg Muffins	Chili Chicken Wings	Authentic Shredded Chicken	The "Squash" Spaghetti
Tues	Delicious Prosciutto Wrapped Cane	Scallions and Eggs Rice Porridge	Corned Beef with Potatoes	Bacon Scramble

			and Red Cabbage	
Wed	Hard Boiled Lazy Devils	Boiled Peanuts	Meat-Loaded Frittata	Brown Sugar and Soy Short Ribs
Thu	Scalloped Potatoes	Flax Coconut Breakfast Pudding	Swedish Party Meatballs	Most Authentic Pepper Steak From The County Side
Fri	The Mediterranean Zoodles With Tuna	Buttery Lobster Tails	Peppery Paprika Poached Eggs	Bacon-Wrapped Carrots
Sat	Mini Turkey Bites	Very Smoky Magical Chicken Sausage Soup	Garlic and Butter Crab Legs	Ham and Cheddar Hash Browns
Sun	Refreshing Turkey Meal	Spicy Corn Cob	Pomegranate Oat Porridge	Garlic and Port Wine Lamb Shanks

Menu for month 10				
	week 1	week 2	week 3	week 4
Mon	Italian Sausages with Peppers	Fine Fennel Shredded Chicken	A Chicken "Faux" Pho	The "fall" Off The Bone Chicken
Tues	Risotto with Shrimp and Eggs	A Beef Stew From The Renaissance	Sloppy Joes	Spicy Shrimp and Tomato Casserole
Wed	Pleasurable Shepherd's Pie	Provoking Goulash	Simple Mashed (Only) Cauliflower	Vegetable Chowder
Thu	Turkey with Cranberries and Sauerkraut	Cinnamon Swirl French Toast with Vanilla	Creamy Haddock with Cheese	Braised Drumsticks For Every Morning
Fri	Delicious Pot of Indian Saag	Lettuce Wrap "Taco" Chicken	Creamy Banana Bread Oatmeal	The Divine Thai Brisket Curry
Sat	Cheese and Mushroom Thyme Oats	Ground Beef, Sauerkraut & Leek	Enchilada Casserole	Protein Packed "Cakes"
Sun	Provoking Goulash	Extremely Elegant Simple Broccoli	Southern Breakfast Cornbread	A Potato Stew With Chard

Menu for month 11				
	week 1	week 2	week 3	week 4
Mon	Tortellini Soup With Basil	The "fall" Off The Bone Chicken	Mexican Rice Casserole	A Very Orange Salmon
Tues	Pepperoni Pizza Pasta	A Simple Bowl Of Mushrooms	Decisive Kalua Pork Meal	Pasta Bolognese
Wed	One Giant Coconut Pancake	Extremely Luxurious Rotisserie Chicken	Early Morning Potato Soup	Rosemary And Veal Stew
Thu	The Excessively Juicy Apple Pork Tenderloins	Sweet Potato and Onion Frittata	Heartwarming Carne Guisada	Ba The Texan Beef Chili con and Egg Sandwich
Fri	French Toast with Bananas and Cinnamon	Chili with Turkey	Heavenly Mana Chicken Stock	A Very Chinese Beef Stew
Sat	Auspicious Mexican Meatloaf	Eggs and Mozzarella with Kale and Hollandaise Sauce	A Touch Of Summer Garden Variety Salad	Perfectly Marinated Seared Artichoke
Sun	Heartwarming Spaghetti Squash and Chicken Marsala	Flavorful Bone Broth	Supremely Spicy And Ravaging Chicken Stew	Very Healthy Green Zoodles

Menu for month 12				
	week 1	week 2	week 3	week 4
Mon	Fancy Spaghetti Squash With Duck Fat Glaze	Chicken with Tomatoes and Sour Cream	Happy Yet Spicy Picadillo	The Largely Skinny Steak Soup
Tues	Meatloaf and BBQ Gravy	Maple and Vanila Quinoa Bowl	The Ultimate Smoked Brisket	Delicious Whole30 Sloppy Joe
Wed	Vegetarian Chili	Original Bone-In Pork Chop	Cherry Dark Chocolate Oat Porridge	An Awkward Garlic Potato
Thu	The Fantastic Potato Gratin	Garlic and Chicken Patties	Dearest Curried Potato Chicken	A Green Soup Worthy For Hulk
Fri	Crazy Lamb Spare Ribs (Overjoyed)	Salsa Eggs	Boiled Peanuts	Swedish Party Meatballs

Sat	Dearest Curried Potato Chicken	Chili Chicken Wings	Eggs with Ham and Gruyere	The Great Potato Casserole Of Beef
Sun	Amazing Lamb Stew	Yet Another Crispy Potato recipe	Saffron and Pork Tenderloin Extreme	Jalapeno Hash with Bacon

Menu for month 13				
	week 1	week 2	week 3	week 4
Mon	Feistily Pounded Carrot Puree	Bacon-Wrapped Carrots	Blessed Ligurian Chicken	Amazing Beef Short Ribs
Tues	Thyme and Rosemary Lambs with Carrots	A Generous Bowl Of Carrot and Kale	Scalloped Potatoes	Beef and Mushroom Stew
Wed	Ravishing Pumpkin Soup	Chili Chicken Curry	The Ultimate Pot Of Rhubarb and Strawberry Compote	Buttery Lobster Tails
Thu	The Perfect Slider Meatballs For Your "Sliders"	Tender Soft Pumpkin Pies	Mini Turkey Bites	Instant Halved Chicken
Fri	Agave Carrot Sticks	Fish and Potatoes Packet	Spicy Corn Cob	Kale and Spinach Risotto
Sat	Thick Pork Chops With Artichoke and Lemon	Instant Eggplant Dip	Mexican Chicken Cacciatore	Garlic and Butter Crab Legs
Sun	A Fine Looking Chili Chicken Verde	Hearty Root Chili	Kale Tahini Hummus	Veggie Cheesy Appetizer

Menu for month 14				
	week 1	week 2	week 3	week 4
Mon	Creamy Herbed Eggs	Authentic Shredded Chicken	The "Squash" Spaghetti	Garlic and Port Wine Lamb Shanks
Tues	Delicious Prosciutto Wrapped Cane	Mashed Cauliflower and Potatoes	Refreshing Turkey Meal	A Chicken "Faux" Pho
Wed	Corned Beef with Potatoes and Red	Brown Sugar and Soy Short Ribs	Simple "Hard" Boiled Eggs	Fine Fennel Shredded Chicken

			Spicy Shrimp and Tomato Casserole	Very Friendly Egg Roll Soup
	Cabbage			
Thu	Cheesy Pepperoni and Spinach Frittata	Breakfast Cinnamon Bread	Spicy Shrimp and Tomato Casserole	Very Friendly Egg Roll Soup
Fri	Turkey with Cranberries and Sauerkraut	Risotto with Shrimp and Eggs	Simplest Meatball Ever	Lettuce Wrap "Taco" Chicken
Sat	Butternut Squash Soup	Provoking Goulash	The "fall" Off The Bone Chicken	The Excessively Juicy Apple Pork Tenderloins
Sun	Decisive Kalua Pork Meal	Instant Scotch Eggs	The Texan Beef Chili	Blueberry Cheesecake Pancake

Menu for month 15				
	week 1	week 2	week 3	week 4
Mon	Mind-Blowing Brussels	Lemony Tapioca Pearls	Simple Instant Hardboiled Eggs	A Rough Patch Potato Roast
Tues	Cheddar and Bean Quessadillas	Mexican Rice Casserole	Pasta Bolognese	Heartwarming Carne Guisada
Wed	Heartwarming Spaghetti Squash and Chicken Marsala	Cheesy Breakfast Bagels	Flavorful Bone Broth	Supremely Spicy And Ravaging Chicken Stew
Thu	Extremely Luxurious Rotisserie Chicken	A Very Orange Salmon	All Natural "Sugar" Free Applesauce	Extremely Healthy Pineapple Pork Chop
Fri	Very Fresh Pinna Colada Chicken!	Thyme and Rosemary Lambs with Carrots	Rosemary And Veal Stew	The Instant Pulled Pork Ragu
Sat	Garlic-y Cuban Pork	Mushroom and Onion Egg Cups	Chili Chicken Curry	A Very Chinese Beef Stew
Sun	Meatloaf and BBQ Gravy	Original Bone-In Pork Chop	An Awkward Garlic Potato	Delicious Whole30 Sloppy Joe

Menu for month 16

	week 1	week 2	week 3	week 4
Mon	Lightly Appetizing Chicken Balls	Carrot and Spinach Sausage-Crusted Quiche	Bacon Thyme Eggs	Blueberry Coconut Porridge
Tues	Sassy Spaghetti Squash With Garlic and Sage	Lovely And Healthy Beets	Garden Quiche	Jalapeno Egg Poppers
Wed	Turmeric Diced Eggs	A Delightful Picnic Salad	Crazy Lamb Spare Ribs (Overjoyed)	Amazing Lamb Stew
Thu	Beef and Mushroom Stew	Blessed Ligurian Chicken	Amazing Beef Short Ribs	Instant Halved Chicken
Fri	Fish and Potatoes Packet	Kale and Spinach Risotto	Thick Pork Chops With Artichoke and Lemon	Mexican Chicken Cacciatore
Sat	Lobster and Cheese Pasta	Juicy and Tender Chicken Drumsticks	Saffron and Pork Tenderloin Extreme	A Fine Looking Chili Chicken Verde
Sun	Hearty Root Chili	The Perfect Slider Meatballs For Your "Sliders"	Chili Chicken Wings	Boiled Peanuts

Menu for month 17

	week 1	week 2	week 3	week 4
Mon	Absolutely Incredible Asparagus Soup	Sausage, Tomato & Corn Breakfast	Classic Cornmeal in the Instant Pot	Espresso Oatmeal
Tues	Astonishing Cauliflower Rice	The Less "Stinky" Onion Soup	Great Morning Guacamole As A Spread	Cheesy Breakfast Steak Rolls
Wed	Instant Breakfast Bread	Multi-Grain Breakfast Porridge	The "Stinking Rose"	Caribbean Beef
Thu	Broccoli Soup With The Blessing Of The Divine	Amazing Pork Chop Of Ghee	Tender Soft Daikon Noodles	Beef Tips in Sauce with Rice

Fri	Tomato Tuna Pasta with Capers	The Very Curious Zuppa Toscana	Very Yummy Chicken Yum Yum (Whole30)	Happy Yet Spicy Picadillo
Sat	The Largely Skinny Steak Soup	Life Altering Chicken Chili Verde 2	Very Subtle Balsamic and Cranberry Chicken	Timmy's Pickled Green Chilies
Sun	Bacon-Wrapped Carrots	Scalloped Potatoes	"Wow" Worthy Ghee Chicken	Very Texan Stylized Beef

		Menu for month 18		
	week 1	week 2	week 3	week 4
Mon	Mashed Assorted Selected Of Veggies	Your New Breakfast Pal "The Boiled Egg"	Spicy Monterey Jack Omelet	Instant Breakfast Burrito
Tues	Feisty Sword Fish And Garlic	Lemony Salmon	Crowd Favorite Lamb Shanks	Rich Fish Stew
Wed	The Authentic Roast and Veggies	Goose with Apples and Raisins	Buffalo Chicken and Potatoes	Very Friendly Ground Beef Chili
Thu	Eggs and Smoked Salmon	An Old Fashioned Baked Potato	Eggplant Olive Spread For Generations To Come	Pulled Pork with Cranberries
Fri	Pork Chops with Apples	Chili Rubbed Salmon	Ultimate Corned Beef Brisket	Yet Another Golden Age Bone Broth
Sat	Classic Mac and Cheese	Juicy Apple and Cherry Breakfast Rice Pudding	Sausage and Ham Omelet	Amazing Beef Bourguignon
Sun	Easy To Make Belizean Chicken Stew	Pulled Apart Pork Carnitas	Very Curious Vietnamese Bo Kho	The Zucchini Pesto Pasta

		Menu for month 19		
	week 1	week 2	week 3	week 4
Mon	Mesmerizing Piccata Potatoes	Acorn Squash With Pork Chops	Innocent Korean Short Ribs	Steak with Veggies

	week 1	week 2	week 3	week 4
Tues	Cordon Bleu Pasta	Pear and Pork Loin Chops	Herb-Loaded Instant Meatloaf	Sweet Pineapple Glazed Ham
Wed	Gentle Giant's Beef Stroganoff	Revolutionary Celery Soup	Tre Colore Frittata	Very Enticing Lemon and Garlic Chicken
Thu	Pumpkin Pie Oatmeal	The Perfect English Stew	Smothered Barbecue Ribs with Cinnamon	Eggplant Tahini Toast with Olives
Fri	The Perfect Mexican Beef	Heart Warming Baby Carrots	Italian Chicken Drumsticks	Gluten Free "Glazed" Chicken Wings
Sat	Simplest Meatball Ever	Taco Pie	A Gentle Early Morning Carrot Soup	Green Kale and Chicken Soup
Sun	Chorizo Pepper Jack Frittata	Supreme Celery and Potato Soup	The Great Indian Goat Curry	Crustless Kale and Tomato Quiche

Menu for month 20			

	week 1	week 2	week 3	week 4
Mon	The Best "Steamed" Chokes	Tuna Noodles with Peas and Cheese	Feta and Leafy Green Egg Cups	Extremely Juicy Apple BBQ Ribs
Tues	Chili Lime Chicken with Rice	Almond and Apricot Oatmeal	The Legendary Chicken Drumstick Soup	Astonishing Vegetable Chicken Breast
Wed	Vegetarian Burger Pattis	Spaghetti Squash "Cooked"	Most Authentic Pepper Steak From The County Side	Sautéed Mushrooms For A Healthy Morning
Thu	A Happy Morning's Picnic Salad 2	Prosciutto Mozzarella Egg Muffins	Snuggly Pineapple Chicken	Mocha Rubbed Delicious Pot Roast
Fri	Pork and Napa Cabbage Soup	Compliant Mayonnaise	Italian Dressing For The "Salads"	Hard Boiled Lazy Devils
Sat	Early Bird Egg Roll Bowl	Scallions and Eggs Rice Porridge	Meat-Loaded Frittata	Buttery Lobster Tails
Sun	Mini Turkey Bites	Spicy Corn Cob	Tilapia and Tomatoes	Garlic and Butter Crab Legs

Menu for month 21

	week 1	week 2	week 3	week 4
Mon	Flax Coconut Breakfast Pudding	The Supreme Pork Shoulder	Authentic Shredded Chicken	The "Squash" Spaghetti
Tues	Corned Beef with Potatoes and Red Cabbage	Peppery Paprika Poached Eggs	Mesmerizing Braised Kale and Carrots	Chard and Mushroom Risotto
Wed	Very Smoky Magical Chicken Sausage Soup	Brown Sugar and Soy Short Ribs	Ham and Cheddar Hash Browns	The Mediterranean Zoodles With Tuna
Thu	Ever So Brilliant Mango Chicken	Pomegranate Oat Porridge	Fine Fennel Shredded Chicken	A Chicken "Faux" Pho
Fri	Turkey with Cranberries and Sauerkraut	Beef Bourguignon	Bacon Scramble	Spicy Shrimp and Tomato Casserole
Sat	A Beef Stew From The Renaissance	Lettuce Wrap "Taco" Chicken	Asian Salmon And Veggies	Italian Sausages with Peppers
Sun	Mexican Rice Casserole	Simple Mashed (Only) Cauliflower	Pasta Bolognese	Heartwarming Spaghetti Squash and Chicken Marsala

Menu for month 22

	week 1	week 2	week 3	week 4
Mon	Braised Drumsticks For Every Morning	Delicious Prosciutto Wrapped Cane	Refreshing Turkey Meal	Sloppy Joes
Tues	Pastrami from the Instant Pot	Pleasurable Shepherd's Pie	Garlic and Port Wine Lamb Shanks	Supremely Spicy And Ravaging Chicken Stew
Wed	Flavorful Bone Broth	Instant Lasagna	Cinnamon Swirl French Toast with Vanilla	Risotto with Shrimp and Eggs
Thu	Cheese and Mushroom Thyme Oats	Extremely Elegant Simple Broccoli	A Salsa Chicken Full Of Magic	Creamy Banana Bread Oatmeal

Fri	Ground Beef, Sauerkraut & Leek	Provoking Goulash	A Potato Stew With Chard	Ketchup Glazed Pork Meatloaf
Sat	A Simple Bowl Of Mushrooms	Enchilada Casserole	Thyme and Rosemary Lambs with Carrots	Tortellini Soup With Basil
Sun	Chili Chicken Curry	Early Morning Potato Soup	Beef and Mushroom Stew	Delicious Pot of Indian Saag

Menu for month 23				
	week 1	week 2	week 3	week 4
Mon	Bacon and Egg Sandwich	One Giant Coconut Pancake	Sweet Potato and Onion Frittata	Heavenly Mana Chicken Stock
Tues	Perfectly Marinated Seared Artichoke	French Toast with Bananas and Cinnamon	Eggs and Mozzarella with Kale and Hollandaise Sauce	Very Healthy Green Zoodles
Wed	Vegetable Chowder	Creamy Haddock with Cheese	The Divine Thai Brisket Curry	Pepperoni Pizza Pasta
Thu	Chili with Turkey	Blessed Ligurian Chicken	Fancy Spaghetti Squash With Duck Fat Glaze	A Touch Of Summer Garden Variety Salad
Fri	Auspicious Mexican Meatloaf	Chicken with Tomatoes and Sour Cream	The Ultimate Smoked Brisket	Maple and Vanila Quinoa Bowl
Sat	Amazing Beef Short Ribs	Instant Halved Chicken	Fish and Potatoes Packet	Kale and Spinach Risotto
Sun	The "fall" Off The Bone Chicken	Decisive Kalua Pork Meal	The Texan Beef Chili	The Excessively Juicy Apple Pork Tenderloins

Menu for month 24				
	week 1	week 2	week 3	week 4
Mon	Cherry Dark Chocolate Oat Porridge	Vegetarian Chili	Garlic and Chicken Patties	The Great Potato Casserole Of Beef
Tues	Heartwarming Carne Guisada	A Green Soup Worthy For Hulk	The Fantastic Potato Gratin	Dearest Curried Potato Chicken

Wed	Ravishing Pumpkin Soup	Extremely Luxurious Rotisserie Chicken	Yet Another Crispy Potato recipe	Salsa Eggs
Thu	Eggs with Ham and Gruyere	Jalapeno Hash with Bacon	Tender Soft Pumpkin Pies	A Very Orange Salmon
Fri	A Very Chinese Beef Stew	Extremely Healthy Pineapple Pork Chop	Feistily Pounded Carrot Puree	Garlic-y Cuban Pork
Sat	Compliant Mayonnaise Recipe	Italian Dressing For The "Salads"	Rosemary And Veal Stew	A Generous Bowl Of Carrot and Kale
Sun	Meatloaf and BBQ Gravy	Thick Pork Chops With Artichoke and Lemon	Veggie Cheesy Appetizer	Mexican Chicken Cacciatore

Menu for month 25				
	week 1	week 2	week 3	week 4
Mon	Fine Fennel Shredded Chicken	The "Squash" Spaghetti	Simplest Meatball Ever	Authentic Shredded Chicken
Tues	Blueberry Cheesecake Pancake for Two	A Chicken "Faux" Pho	Corned Beef with Potatoes and Red Cabbage	Instant Scotch Eggs
Wed	Lettuce Wrap "Taco" Chicken	Protein Packed "Cakes"	Spicy Shrimp and Tomato Casserole	Brown Sugar and Soy Short Ribs
Thu	Southern Breakfast Cornbread	Mexican Rice Casserole	Creamy Herbed Eggs	Turkey with Cranberries and Sauerkraut
Fri	Flavorful Bone Broth	Mashed Cauliflower and Potatoes	Pasta Bolognese	Simple "Hard" Boiled Eggs
Sat	Very Friendly Egg Roll Soup	Supremely Spicy And Ravaging Chicken Stew	Butternut Squash Soup	Heartwarming Spaghetti Squash and Chicken Marsala
Sun	Delicious Prosciutto Wrapped Cane	Cheesy Pepperoni and Spinach Frittata	Refreshing Turkey Meal	Breakfast Cinnamon Bread

Menu for month 26				
	week 1	week 2	week 3	week 4

233

Mon	Mind-Blowing Brussels	Garlic and Port Wine Lamb Shanks	Risotto with Shrimp and Eggs	Provoking Goulash
Tues	The "fall" Off The Bone Chicken	Lemony Tapioca Pearls	Decisive Kalua Pork Meal	The Texan Beef Chili
Wed	Cheddar and Bean Quessadillas	The Excessively Juicy Apple Pork Tenderloins	Simple Instant Hardboiled Eggs	Heartwarming Carne Guisada
Thu	Extremely Luxurious Rotisserie Chicken	Cheesy Breakfast Bagels	A Very Orange Salmon	A Rough Patch Potato Roast
Fri	Very Fresh Pinna Colada Chicken!	Extremely Healthy Pineapple Pork Chop	All Natural "Sugar" Free Applesauce	Blessed Ligurian Chicken
Sat	Thyme and Rosemary Lambs with Carrots	Mushroom and Onion Egg Cups	Beef and Mushroom Stew	The Instant Pulled Pork Ragu
Sun	Carrot and Spinach Sausage-Crusted Quiche	Chili Chicken Curry	Lightly Appetizing Chicken Balls	Amazing Beef Short Ribs

Menu for month 27				
	week 1	week 2	week 3	week 4
Mon	Instant Halved Chicken	Rosemary And Veal Stew	A Very Chinese Beef Stew	Meatloaf and BBQ Gravy
Tues	An Awkward Garlic Potato	Fish and Potatoes Packet	Kale and Spinach Risotto	Original Bone-In Pork Chop
Wed	Mexican Chicken Cacciatore	Delicious Whole30 Sloppy Joe	Crazy Lamb Spare Ribs (Overjoyed)	Thick Pork Chops With Artichoke and Lemon
Thu	Bacon Thyme Eggs	Lobster and Cheese Pasta	Amazing Lamb Stew	Saffron and Pork Tenderloin Extreme
Fri	Blueberry Coconut Porridge	Sassy Spaghetti Squash With Garlic and Sage	Juicy and Tender Chicken Drumsticks	Lovely And Healthy Beets
Sat	Broccoli Soup With The Blessing Of The Divine	Garlic-y Cuban Pork	Garden Quiche	Caribbean Beef

			A Delightful	Absolutely Incredible
Sun	Jalapeno Egg Poppers	Turmeric Diced Eggs	Picnic Salad	Asparagus Soup

Menu for month 28

	week 1	week 2	week 3	week 4
Mon	Sausage, Tomato & Corn Breakfast	Classic Cornmeal in the Instant Pot	Espresso Oatmeal	Astonishing Cauliflower Rice
Tues	The Less "Stinky" Onion Soup	Great Morning Guacamole As A Spread	Cheesy Breakfast Steak Rolls	Instant Breakfast Bread
Wed	Amazing Pork Chop Of Ghee	Tender Soft Daikon Noodles	Beef Tips in Sauce with Rice	Tomato Tuna Pasta with Capers
Thu	The Very Curious Zuppa Toscana	Very Yummy Chicken Yum Yum (Whole30)	The Authentic Roast and Veggies	Goose with Apples and Raisins
Fri	Buffalo Chicken and Potatoes	Pulled Pork with Cranberries	A Fine Looking Chili Chicken Verde	Hearty Root Chili
Sat	The Perfect Slider Meatballs For Your "Sliders"	Happy Yet Spicy Picadillo	The Largely Skinny Steak Soup	Life Altering Chicken Chili Verde 2
Sun	Very Subtle Balsamic and Cranberry Chicken	Timmy's Pickled Green Chilies	"Wow" Worthy Ghee Chicken	Very Texan Stylized Beef

Menu for month 29

	week 1	week 2	week 3	week 4
Mon	Feisty Sword Fish And Garlic	Crowd Favorite Lamb Shanks	Very Friendly Ground Beef Chili	Chili Rubbed Salmon
Tues	Ultimate Corned Beef Brisket	Yet Another Golden Age Bone Broth	Easy To Make Belizean Chicken Stew	The Zucchini Pesto Pasta
Wed	Pork Chops with Apples	Pulled Apart Pork Carnitas	Amazing Beef Bourguignon	Very Curious Vietnamese Bo Kho

Thu	Classic Mac and Cheese	Lemony Salmon	Rich Fish Stew	Acorn Squash With Pork Chops
Fri	Innocent Korean Short Ribs	Steak with Veggies	Multi-Grain Breakfast Porridge	The "Stinking Rose"
Sat	Mashed Assorted Selected Of Veggies	Your New Breakfast Pal "The Boiled Egg"	Spicy Monterey Jack Omelet	Instant Breakfast Burrito
Sun	Eggs and Smoked Salmon	An Old Fashioned Baked Potato	Eggplant Olive Spread For Generations To Come	Sausage and Ham Omelet

Menu for month 30			
	week 1	week 2	week 3	week 4
Mon	Juicy Apple and Cherry Breakfast Rice Pudding	Cordon Bleu Pasta	Herb-Loaded Instant Meatloaf	Sweet Pineapple Glazed Ham
Tues	Smothered Barbecue Ribs with Cinnamon	Mesmerizing Piccata Potatoes	Gentle Giant's Beef Stroganoff	The Perfect English Stew
Wed	Eggplant Tahini Toast with Olives	Taco Pie	Pear and Pork Loin Chops	Chili Lime Chicken with Rice
Thu	Extremely Juicy Apple BBQ Ribs	Pumpkin Pie Oatmeal	Tuna Noodles with Peas and Cheese	Tre Colore Frittata
Fri	Revolutionary Celery Soup	Astonishing Vegetable Chicken Breast	Heart Warming Baby Carrots	Spaghetti Squash "Cooked"
Sat	Crustless Kale and Tomato Quiche	Chorizo Pepper Jack Frittata	Very Enticing Lemon and Garlic Chicken	A Gentle Early Morning Carrot Soup
Sun	Simplest Meatball Ever	The Great Indian Goat Curry	Supreme Celery and Potato Soup	The Perfect Mexican Beef

Menu for month 31			
	week 1	week 2	week 3	week 4

	week 1	week 2	week 3	week 4
Mon	Chili Chicken Wings	Italian Chicken Drumsticks	The Best "Steamed" Chokes	Almond and Apricot Oatmeal
Tues	The Legendary Chicken Drumstick Soup	Boiled Peanuts	Gluten Free "Glazed" Chicken Wings	Feta and Leafy Green Egg Cups
Wed	Sautéed Mushrooms For A Healthy Morning	Snuggly Pineapple Chicken	Mocha Rubbed Delicious Pot Roast	Green Kale and Chicken Soup
Thu	A Happy Morning's Picnic Salad 2	Bacon-Wrapped Carrots	Pork and Napa Cabbage Soup	Swedish Party Meatballs
Fri	Early Bird Egg Roll Bowl	Prosciutto Mozzarella Egg Muffins	Scallions and Eggs Rice Porridge	Meat-Loaded Frittata
Sat	Most Authentic Pepper Steak From The County Side	Cordon Bleu Pasta	Vegetarian Burger Pattis	Tilapia and Tomatoes
Sun	The Supreme Pork Shoulder	Mesmerizing Braised Kale and Carrots	Chard and Mushroom Risotto	Ever So Brilliant Mango Chicken

Menu for month 32				
	week 1	week 2	week 3	week 4
Mon	Beef Bourguignon	Asian Salmon And Veggies	Pastrami from the Instant Pot	Instant Lasagna
Tues	A Salsa Chicken Full Of Magic	Ketchup Glazed Pork Meatloaf	Delicious Pot of Indian Saag	Ground Beef, Sauerkraut & Leek
Wed	Enchilada Casserole	Sloppy Joes	Vegetable Chowder	Delicious Prosciutto Wrapped Cane
Thu	Refreshing Turkey Meal	Garlic and Port Wine Lamb Shanks	Risotto with Shrimp and Eggs	Provoking Goulash
Fri	The "fall" Off The Bone Chicken	Decisive Kalua Pork Meal	The Texan Beef Chili	The Excessively Juicy Apple Pork Tenderloins
Sat	Hard Boiled Lazy Devils	Flax Coconut Breakfast Pudding	Peppery Paprika Poached Eggs	Ham and Cheddar Hash Browns

Sun	The Mediterranean Zoodles With Tuna	Very Smoky Magical Chicken Sausage Soup	Pomegranate Oat Porridge	Bacon Scramble

Menu for month 33				
	week 1	week 2	week 3	week 4
Mon	Italian Sausages with Peppers	A Beef Stew From The Renaissance	Creamy Haddock with Cheese	The Divine Thai Brisket Curry
Tues	Pepperoni Pizza Pasta	Chili with Turkey	Simple Mashed (Only) Cauliflower	Braised Drumsticks For Every Morning
Wed	Pleasurable Shepherd's Pie	Cinnamon Swirl French Toast with Vanilla	Creamy Banana Bread Oatmeal	Cheese and Mushroom Thyme Oats
Thu	Extremely Elegant Simple Broccoli	A Touch Of Summer Garden Variety Salad	Auspicious Mexican Meatloaf	Chicken with Tomatoes and Sour Cream
Fri	The Ultimate Smoked Brisket	A Potato Stew With Chard	Vegetarian Chili	Heartwarming Carne Guisada
Sat	Extremely Luxurious Rotisserie Chicken	A Very Orange Salmon	Tortellini Soup With Basil	Extremely Healthy Pineapple Pork Chop
Sun	Garlic-y Cuban Pork	Scalloped Potatoes	Buttery Lobster Tails	Mini Turkey Bites

Menu for month 34				
	week 1	week 2	week 3	week 4
Mon	Rosemary And Veal Stew	A Very Chinese Beef Stew	Meatloaf and BBQ Gravy	Original Bone-In Pork Chop
Tues	A Simple Bowl Of Mushrooms	Early Morning Potato Soup	Bacon and Egg Sandwich	One Giant Coconut Pancake
Wed	Sweet Potato and Onion Frittata	An Awkward Garlic Potato	Heavenly Mana Chicken Stock	Perfectly Marinated Seared Artichoke
Thu	Amazing Lamb Stew	French Toast with Bananas and Cinnamon	Delicious Whole30 Sloppy Joe	Eggs and Mozzarella with Kale and

				Hollandaise Sauce
Fri	Garlic and Chicken Patties	Saffron and Pork Tenderloin Extreme	The Great Potato Casserole Of Beef	Crazy Lamb Spare Ribs (Overjoyed)
Sat	Dearest Curried Potato Chicken	Yet Another Crispy Potato recipe	Ravishing Pumpkin Soup	Tender Soft Pumpkin Pies
Sun	A Fine Looking Chili Chicken Verde	Hearty Root Chili	The Perfect Slider Meatballs For Your "Sliders"	Happy Yet Spicy Picadillo

Menu for month 35				
	week 1	week 2	week 3	week 4
Mon	Authentic Shredded Chicken	Very Healthy Green Zoodles	The "Squash" Spaghetti	Corned Beef with Potatoes and Red Cabbage
Tues	Maple and Vanila Quinoa Bowl	Brown Sugar and Soy Short Ribs	Fancy Spaghetti Squash With Duck Fat Glaze	Fine Fennel Shredded Chicken
Wed	A Chicken "Faux" Pho	Cherry Dark Chocolate Oat Porridge	Spicy Shrimp and Tomato Casserole	Turkey with Cranberries and Sauerkraut
Thu	The Fantastic Potato Gratin	Lettuce Wrap "Taco" Chicken	A Green Soup Worthy For Hulk	Mexican Rice Casserole
Fri	Heartwarming Spaghetti Squash and Chicken Marsala	Salsa Eggs	Pasta Bolognese	Eggs with Ham and Gruyere
Sat	Jalapeno Hash with Bacon	Flavorful Bone Broth	Feistily Pounded Carrot Puree	Beef and Mushroom Stew
Sun	Supremely Spicy And Ravaging Chicken Stew	Thyme and Rosemary Lambs with Carrots	Chili Chicken Curry	Blessed Ligurian Chicken

Menu for month 36				
	week 1	week 2	week 3	week 4

239

				A Fine Looking Chili Chicken Verde
Mon	A Generous Bowl Of Carrot and Kale	Beef Tips in Sauce with Rice	Caribbean Beef	
Tues	Hearty Root Chili	The Ultimate Pot Of Rhubarb and Strawberry Compote	The Perfect Slider Meatballs For Your "Sliders"	Broccoli Soup With The Blessing Of The Divine
Wed	Fish and Potatoes Packet	The Largely Skinny Steak Soup	Amazing Beef Short Ribs	Happy Yet Spicy Picadillo
Thu	Life Altering Chicken Chili Verde	Kale and Spinach Risotto	Timmy's Pickled Green Chilies	Instant Halved Chicken
Fri	Lobster and Cheese Pasta	Amazing Pork Chop Of Ghee	Thick Pork Chops With Artichoke and Lemon	Very Subtle Balsamic and Cranberry Chicken
Sat	"Wow" Worthy Ghee Chicken	Juicy and Tender Chicken Drumsticks	Tender Soft Daikon Noodles	Mexican Chicken Cacciatore
Sun	Very Texan Stylized Beef	Feisty Sword Fish And Garlic	Crowd Favorite Lamb Shanks	Very Friendly Ground Beef Chili

Conclusion

I can't express how honored I am to think that you found my book interesting and informative enough to read it all through to the end.

I thank you again for purchasing this book and I hope that you had as much fun reading it as I had writing it.

I bid you farewell and encourage you to move forward with your amazing Whole30 journey with the Instant Pot!

Appendix

General Instant Pot Cooking Timetable For Fruits

Fruits	Cooking Time For Fresh Fruits	Cooking Time For Dried Fruits
Slices of Apples	2 to 3	3 to 4
Whole Apples	3 to 4	4 to 6
Halves of Whole Portions Of Apricots	2 to 3	3 to 4
Normal Peaches	2 to 3	4 to 5
Whole pieces of Pears	3 to 4	4 to 6
Halves or Slices of Pears	2 to 3	4 to 5
Whole Prunes	2 to 3	4 to 5
Whole Raisins	N/A	4 to 5

General Instant Pot Cooking Timetable For Vegetables

Vegetable	Cooking Time For Fresh Fruits	Cooking Time For Dried Fruits
Whole Artichokes with only leaves trimmed up	9 to 11	11 to 13

Hearts of Artichokes	4 to 5	5 to 6
Whole or cut up Asparagus	1 to 2	2 to 3
Green or Yellow Beans, Whole	1 to 2	2 to 3
Whole portions of beets with small roots	11 to 13	13 to 15
Whole portions of beets with large roots	20 to 25	25 to 30
Florets of Broccoli	2 to 3	3 to 4
Stalks of Broccoli	3 to 4	4 to 5
Whole pieces of Brussels Sprouts	3 to 4	4 to 5
Shredded cabbage of either red, green or purple color	2 to 3	3 to 4
Cabbage wedges of either red, green or purple color	3 to 4	4 to 5
Shredded or sliced up carrots	1 to 2	2 to 3
Whole or chunked up Carrots	2 to 3	3 to 4
Chunks of Celery	2 to 3	3 to 4
Whole Collards	4 to 5	5 to 6
Kernels Of Corn	1 to 2	2 to 3
On The Cob "Corns"	3 to 4	4 to 5
Slices of Chunks Of Eggplants	2 to 3	3 to 4
Whole Endive	1 to 2	2 to 3
Chopped up Escarole	1 to 2	2 to 3

Whole pieces of Green Beans	2 to 3	3 to 4
Greens such as Collards, Spinach etc.	3 to 6	4 to 7
Whole Leeks	2 to 4	3 to 5
Assorted Vegetables	2 to 3	3 to 4
Whole Okra	2 to 3	3 to 4
Sliced Up Onions	2 to 3	3 to 4
Sliced up Parsnips	1 to 2	2 to 3
Chunks of Parsnips	2 to 4	4 to 6
Peas in Pod	1 to 2	2 to 3
Green Peas	1 to 2	2 to 3
Cubes of Potatoes	7 to 9	9 to 11
Whole portions of Baby Potatoes	10 to 12	12 to 14
Whole portions of Large potatoes	12 to 15	15 to 19
Small Slices or Chunks of Pumpkins	4 to 5	6 to 7
Large slices or chunks of Pumpkins	8 to 10	10 to 14
Slices of Rutabaga	3 to 5	4 to 6
Chunks of Rutabaga	4 to 6	6 to 8
Whole Spinach	1 to 2	3 to 4
Slices or chunks of squash acorns	6 to 7	8 to 9

Slices of chunks Butternut Squash	8 to 10	10 to 12
Cubes of Sweet Potatoes	7 to 9	9 to 11
Small sized whole sweet potatoes	10 to 12	12 to 14
Large sized whole sweet potatoes	12 to 15	15 to 19
Slices or Chunks of Sweet Peppers	1 to 3	2 to 4
Quarters of Tomatoes	2 to 3	4 to 5
Whole pieces of Tomatoes	3 to 5	5 to 7
Chunks of Turnips	2 to 4	4 to 6
Cubes of Yam	7 to 9	9 to 11
Small sized whole Yam	10 to 12	12 to 14
Large sized whole Yam	12 to 15	15 to 19
Slices of chunks of Zucchini	2 to 3	3 to 4

General Instant Pot Cooking Timetable For Fish and Seafood

Seafood and Fish	Cooking Time For Freshly Caught Fish	Cooking Time For Frozen Fish
Whole Crabs	3 to 4	5 to 6
Whole Fish Such as Trout or Snapper	5 to 6	7 to 10

Fillets of Fish	2 to 3	3 to 4
Finely Prepared Fish Steaks	3 to 4	4 to 6
Whole Lobsters	3 to 4	4 to 6
Whole Mussels	2 to 3	4 to 5
Soup or Stock or Fish/Seafood	6 to 7	7 to 9
General Shrimp or Prawn	1 to 2	2 to 3

General Instant Pot Cooking Timetable For Meat

Meat	Time Require For Cooking The Meat
Stew Meat Of Beef	15 to 20
Meat Balls Of Beef	10 to15
Dressed Beef Meat	20 to 25
Large Sized Chuck Blade, Roast, Rump, Steak, or Brisket of Beef	35 to 40
Small Chunks of Chuck Blade, Roast, Rump, Steak, or Brisket of Beef	25 to 30
Ribs of Beef	25 to 30
Shanks Of Beef	25 to 30
Oxtails of Beef	40 to 50
Breast Of Chicken	8 to 10
Whole Sized Chicken	20 to 25
Boneless Chickens	10 to 15
Drumsticks, legs or Thigh Of Chicken	10 to 15

Whole portion of Cornish Hen	10 to 15
Boneless Duck	10 to 12
Whole Portion Of Duck	25 to 30
Sliced up Ham	9 to 12
Picnic Shoulder Of Ham	25 to 30
Cubes Of Lamb Meat	10 to15
Stew Meat Of Lamb	10 to15
Legs Of Lamb	35 to 45
Traditional Pheasant Meat	20 to 25
Simple Pork Loin Roast	55 to 60
Simple Pork Butt Roast	45 to 50
Ribs Of Pork	20 to 25
Boneless Breast Meat Of Turkey	15 to 20
Whole Turkey Breast Meat With Bone	25 to 30
Drumsticks Of Turkey	15 to 20
Chops Of Veal	5 to 8
Roast Of Veal	35 to 45
Whole Quail Meat	8 to 10

Made in the USA
Middletown, DE
30 October 2018